John Griffith London (born **John Griffith Chaney**; January 12, 1876 – November 22, 1916) was an American novelist, journalist, and social activist. A pioneer in the world of commercial magazine fiction, he was one of the first writers to become a worldwide celebrity and earn a large fortune from writing. He was also an innovator in the genre that would later become known as science fiction. His most famous works include The Call of the Wild and White Fang, both set in the Klondike Gold Rush, as well as the short stories "To Build a Fire", "An Odyssey of the North", and "Love of Life". He also wrote about the South Pacific in stories such as "The Pearls of Parlay" and "The Heathen". London was part of the radical literary group "The Crowd" in San Francisco and a passionate advocate of unionization, socialism, and the rights of workers. He wrote several powerful works dealing with these topics, such as his dystopian novel The Iron Heel, his non-fiction exposé The People of the Abyss, and The War of the Classes. (Source: Wikipedia)

Literary works:
The Cruise of the Dazzler (1902)
A Daughter of the Snows (1902)
The Call of the Wild (1903)
The Kempton-Wace Letters (1903)
The Sea-Wolf (1904)
The Game (1905)
White Fang (1906)
Before Adam (1907)
The Iron Heel (1908)
Martin Eden (1909)
Burning Daylight (1910)
Adventure (1911)
The Scarlet Plague (1912)
A Son of the Sun (1912)
The Abysmal Brute (1913)
The Valley of the Moon (1913)

THRONE CLASSICS

SCORN OF WOMEN
JACK LONDON

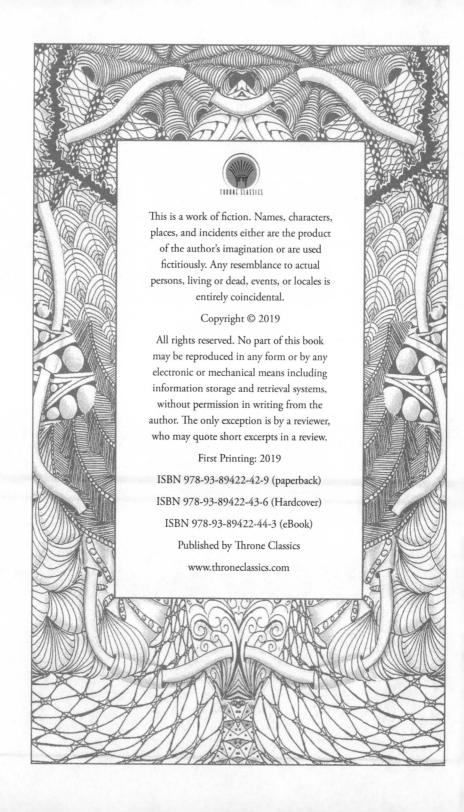

Copyright © 2019

First Printing: 2019

ISBN 978-93-89422-42-9 (paperback)

ISBN 978-93-89422-43-6 (Hardcover)

ISBN 978-93-89422-44-3 (eBook)

Published by Throne Classics

www.throneclassics.com

Contents

SCORN OF WOMEN

Time of play, 1897, Dawson, Northwest Territory. It occurs in thirteen hours.

Freda Moloof............A dancer.

Floyd Vanderlip.........An Eldorado king.

Loraine Lisznayi........A Hungarian.

Captain Eppingwell......United States government agent.

Mrs. Eppingwell.........His wife.

Flossie.................Engaged to marry Floyd Vanderlip

Sitka Charley...........An Indian dog-driver.

Dave Harney.............An Eldorado king.

Prince..................A mining engineer.

Mrs. McFee..............Whose business is morals.

Minnie..................Maid to Freda Moloof.

Dog-punchers, couriers, miners, Indians, mounted police, clerks, etc.

FREDA MOLOOF. A Greek girl and a dancer. Speaks perfect English, but withal has that slight, indefinable foreign touch of accent. Good figure, willowy, yet not too slender. Of indeterminate age, possibly no more than twenty-five. Her furs the most magnificent in all the Yukon country from Chilcoot to St. Michael's, her name common on the lips of men.

FLOYD VANDERLIP. An Eldorado king, worth a couple of millions. Simple, elemental, almost childish in his emotions. But a brave man, and masculine; a man who has done a man's work in the world. Has caressed more shovel-handles than women's hands. Big-muscled, big-bodied, ingenuous-faced; the sort of a man whom women of the right sort can tie into knots.

LORAINE LISZNAYI. A Hungarian, reputed to be wealthy, and to be travelling in the Klondike for pleasure and love of adventure. Past the flush of youth, and with fair success feigning youth. In the first stages of putting flesh upon her erstwhile plumpness. Dark-eyed, a flashing, dazzling brunette, with a cosmopolitan reputation earned in a day when she posed in the studios of artist-queens and received at her door the cards of cardinals and princes.

CAPTAIN EPPINGWELL. Special agent for the United States government.

MRS. EPPINGWELL. His wife. Twenty-five to twenty-eight years of age. Of the cold order of women, possessing sanity, and restraint, and control. Brown hair, demi-blond type, oval-faced, with cameo-like features. The kind of a woman who is not painfully good, but who acts upon principle and who knows always just what she is doing.

FLOSSIE. Eighteen or nineteen years of age. Of the soft and clinging kind, with pretty, pouting lips, blow-away hair, and eyes full of the merry shallows of life. Engaged to marry Floyd Vanderlip.

PRINCE. A young mining engineer. A good fellow, a man's man.

MRS. MCFEE. Near to forty, Scotch accent, sharp-featured, and unbeautiful, with an eager nose that leads her into the affairs of others. So painfully good that it hurts.

SITKA CHARLEY. An Indian dog-puncher, who has come into the warm and sat by the fires of the white man until he is somewhat as one of them. Should not be much shorter than Vanderlip and Captain Eppingwell.

DAVE HARNEY. An Eldorado king, also a Yankee, with a fondness for sugar and a faculty for sharp dealing. Is tall, lean, loose-jointed. Walks with a shambling gait. Speaks slowly, with a drawl.

MINNIE. (Maid to Freda.) A cool, impassive young woman.

POLICEMAN. A young fellow, with small blond mustache. An Englishman, brave, cool, but easily embarrassed. Though he says "Sorry" frequently, he is never for an instant afraid.

ACT I—ALASKA COMPANY'S STORE AT DAWSON

Scene. *Alaska Commercial Company's store at Dawson. It is eleven o'clock of a cold winter morning. In front, on the left, a very large wood-burning stove. Beside the stove is a woodbox filled with firewood. Farther back, on left, a door with sign on it, "Private." On right, door, a street entrance; alongside are wisp-brooms for brushing snow from moccasins. In the background a long counter running full length of room with just space at either end for ingress or egress. Large gold-scales rest upon counter. Behind counter equally long rows of shelves, broken in two places by ordinary small-paned house-windows. Windows are source of a dim, gray light. Doors, window-frames, and sashes are of rough, unstained pine boards. Shelves practically empty, with here and there upon them an article of hardware (such as pots, pans, and tea-kettles), or of dry-goods (such as pasteboard boxes and bolts of cloth). The walls of the store are of logs stuffed between with brown moss. On counter, furs, moccasins, mittens, and blankets, piled up or spread out for inspection. In front of counter many snow-shoes, picks, shovels, axes, gold-pans, axe-handles, and oblong sheet-iron Yukon stoves. The feature most notable is the absence of foodstuffs in any considerable quantity. On shelves a few tins of mushrooms, a few bottles of olives.*

About the stove, backs to the stove and hands behind their backs, clad in mackinaw suits, mittens dangling from around their necks at ends of leather thongs, ear-flaps of fur caps raised, are several miners. Prince stands by stove An Indian is replenishing the fire with great chunks of wood. Mounted police pass in and out. Sitka Charley is examining snow-shoes, bending and testing them. Behind the counter are several clerks, one of whom is waiting upon a bearded miner near end of counter to right.

MINER

(Pathetically.) No flour?

CLERK

(Shakes head.)

MINER

(Increased pathos.)

No beans?

CLERK

(Shakes head as before.)

MINER

(Supreme pathos.)

No sugar?

CLERK

(Coming from behind counter and approaching stove, visibly irritated, shaking his head violently; midway he encounters Miner, who retreats backward before him.)

No! No! No! I tell you no! No flour, no beans, no sugar, nothing!

(Warms his hands over stove and glares ferociously at Miner.)

(Dave Harney enters from right, brushes snow from moccasins, and walks across to stove. He is tall and lean, has a loose-jointed, shambling gait, and listens interestedly to Clerk and Miner. He evinces a desire to speak, but his mustached mouth is so iced-up that he cannot open it. He bends over stove to thaw the ice.)

MINER

(To Clerk, with growing anger.)

It's all very well for your playing the high an' lofty, you sneakin' little counter-jumper. But we all know what your damned Company is up to. You're holdin' grub for a rise, that's what you're doin'. Famine prices is your game.

CLERK

Look at the shelves, man! Look at them!

MINER

How about the warehouses, eh? Stacked to the roof with grub!

CLERK

They're not.

MINER

I suppose you'll say they're empty.

CLERK

They're not. But what little grub's in them belongs to the sour-doughs who filed their orders last spring and summer before ever you thought of coming into the country. And even the sourdoughs are scaled down, cut clean in half. Now shut up. I don't want to hear any more from you. You newcomers needn't think you're going to run this country, because you ain't.

(Turning his hack on Miner.)

Damned cheechawker!

MINER

(Breaking down and showing fear, not of Clerk, but of famine.)

But good heavens, man, what am I to do? I haven't fifty pounds of flour for the whole winter.

I can pay for my grub if you'll sell it to me. You can't leave me starve!

DAVE HARNEY

(Tearing the last chunk oj ice from mustache and sending it rattling to the floor. He speaks with a drawl.)

Aw, you tenderfeet make me tired. I never seen the beat of you critters. Better men than you have starved in this country, an' they didn't make no bones about it neither—they was all bones I calkilate. What do you think

13

this is? A Sunday picnic? Jes' come in, eh? An' you're clean scairt. Look at me—old-timer, sir, a sour-dough, an' proud of it! I come into this country before there was any blamed Company, fished for my breakfast, an' hunted my supper. An' when the fish didn't bite an' they wa'n't any game, jes' cinched my belt tighter an' hiked along, livin' on salmon-bellies and rabbit tracks an' eatin' my moccasins.

(Jubilantly.)

Oh, I tell you this is the country that'll take the saleratus out of you!

(Miner, awed by being face to face with an old-timer, withers up during harangue, and at finish shrinks behind other miners, and from there makes exit to right.)

(Drawing paper from pocket and presenting it.)

Now lookee here, Mister Clerk, what'd you call that?

CLERK

(Glancing perfunctorily at paper.)

Grub contract.

DAVE HARNEY

What's it stand for?

CLERK

(Wearily.)

One thousand pounds of grub.

DAVE HARNEY

An' how much sugar?

CLERK

One thousand pounds of grub.

DAVE HARNEY

Say it again.

CLERK

(Looking for item on paper and reading.) Seventy-five pounds.

DAVE HARNEY

(Triumphantly.)

That's the way I made it out. I thought my eyes was all right.

CLERK

(After a pause.)

Well?

DAVE HARNEY

Well, that mangy little cuss around at the warehouse said I could only get five hundred on that piece of paper, an' nary sugar. What's that mean?

CLERK

It means five hundred pounds and no sugar. Scale-down went into effect to-day. Orders.

DAVE HARNEY

(Wistfully.)

An' nary sugar?

CLERK

Nary sugar.

DAVE HARNEY

That grub's mine, an' that sugar. I paid for it last spring. Weighed my dust in on them scales there.

CLERK

Can't help it. Orders.

DAVE HARNEY

(Wistfully.)

An' nary sugar?

CLERK

Nary sugar.

DAVE HARNEY

(Meditatively, in low voice.)

Curious, ain't it? Mighty curious—me ownin' two five-hundred-foot Eldorado claims, with five million if I'm wuth a cent, an' no sweetenin' for my coffee or mush.

('Whirling upon Clerk in sudden wrath, Clerk retreating wearily to behind counter.)

Why, gosh dang it! this country kin go to blazes! I'll sell out! I'll quit it cold! I'll—I'll—go back to the States! I'll—I'll—see the management!

(Strides rapidly toward door to left.)

CLERK

Hold on!

(Dave Harney stops.)

The boss is busy. Vanderlip's with'm.

DAVE HARNEY

He's buckin' the sugar proposition, too, eh? Clerk

No, he ain't.

DAVE HARNEY

Then here goes. Dave Harney don't wait on Vanderlip or any other man.

(Jerks open door marked "Private.")

(Vanderlip appears in doorway, just entering.)

VANDERLIP

Hello, Dave. What's the rush?

DAVE HARNEY

Hello, Vanderlip. Got any sugar to sell?

VANDERLIP

No, but I want to buy—

DAVE HARNEY

(Interrupting.)

No sugar, you can't do business with me.

(Rushes through door, slamming it after him.)

(General laugh from miners about stove. Clerk throws up his arms despairingly.)

(Vanderlip looks backward through door, which he pulls open for a moment, and laughs at Dave Harney.)

(Loraine Lisznayi enters from right and pauses at door to brush snow from moccasins.)

VANDERLIP

(Sees Loraine Lisznayi, starts across to meet her, but stops midway to speak hurriedly to Sitka Charley.)

How about those dogs, Charley?

SITKA CHARLEY

I get um all right by and by.

VANDERLIP

I want them right away, to-day.

SITKA CHARLEY

Yesterday you tell me to-morrow.

VANDERLIP

To-day, I tell you to-day. Never mind the price. I must have them—good dogs. Tonight, twelve o'clock, have them down at the water-hole all ready, harnesses, grub, everything in shape. And you're to drive them down river for me. Sure?

SITKA CHARLEY

Sure.

VANDERLIP

(Over his shoulder as he continues to cross to right.)

Never mind the price. I must have them.

(Crosses on over to right to Loraine Lisznayi, an expression of joy on his face. Sweeps off his Fur cap and shakes her hand.)

LORAINE

You must do better than that. Had there been a woman here, your face would have given everything away.

VANDERLIP

I can't help the gladness getting into my face, Loraine.

LORAINE

Don't call me Loraine. Somebody might hear. And we can't be too careful. And you mustn't talk but for a moment, Floyd.

VANDERLIP

(Grinning broadly.)

There you go, calling me Floyd. Somebody might hear. But who's afraid? I'm not. Let 'em hear. I'm glad of it! Proud of it that you're mine. The dearest little woman in the world, and mine, all mine!

LORAINE

(Glancing furtively about and finding that nobody is paying any attention.)

Hush, dear. Wait until we are safely away, and then I shall be proud before all the world to have you proud of me. You are such a man! Such a man!

VANDERLIP

Just wait until I get you into that Mediterranean palace. We'll make 'em sit up with this Klondike gold of ours. People don't know how rich I am, Loraine. Nor do you. I've got pay-claims over on Dominion Creek nobody dreams of, and—

LORAINE

I don't care how much you've got, or how little. It's you, you big, big man, you, my hero, that I care for. You'll grace a palace like a prince, and I've known a few princes, too.

VANDERLIP

And queens, too, didn't you say?

LORAINE

Yes, and queens, too. And they will be proud and glad to know you. They don't have men like you over there—real men. You'll create a sensation.

VANDERLIP

(Anxiously.)

But this living in palaces—sort of softening and fattening, ain't it? I don't like fat.

(Looks her over critically.)

You don't incline that way, do you?

LORAINE

(Laughing.)

You foolish, dear man, of course not. Do I look it?

VANDERLIP

(Slowly.)

Well, you look round—and plump.

LORAINE

I've always been plump like this. I'm like my mother. She was that way. She never got stout, and neither shall I.

VANDERLIP

(Anxiety going out of face, being replaced by satisfaction.)

Oh, you're all right, Loraine, you bet.

LORAINE

But you must leave me now, Floyd. Somebody may come in at any moment. Besides, I've a few little things to buy for our journey.

VANDERLIP

And they're fixing my money for me in there.

(Nodding toward door at lejt. Loraine betrays keen and involuntary interest). Letters of credit, you know, and all that. Can't carry much dust. Too heavy. And by the way, keep the weight down. Don't buy too many little things. Dogs are dogs, and they can only haul so much.

LORAINE

Only enough for me to be comfortable.

VANDERLIP

A woman needs so almighty much to be comfortable. But it'll be all right. Two sleds'll carry us, no matter how comfortable you make yourself. Bring plenty of foot-gear, moccasins, and stockings, and such things. And be at the water-hole at midnight with your whole outfit. Be sure that Indian of yours has enough dog food. I'll get my dogs to-day some time.

LORAINE

Which water-hole?

VANDERLIP

The one by the hospital. Don't make a mistake and go to the other one. It's way out of the way.

LORAINE

And now you simply must leave me. And you mustn't see me again to-day—not till midnight, at the water-hole, by the hospital. You know I can scarcely bear to have you out of my sight. But these women—oh, they are such suspicious creatures!

VANDERLIP

Good-by, then, until to-night.

(Turns to go toward left.)

LORAINE

(Softly.)

Floyd!

(Vanderlip turns back.)

You must go to the ball to-night. I've begged off, but you must go. It will avert any possible suspicion.

VANDERLIP

I was going anyway, just to drop in for a while. I—that is, you see—I promised Mrs. Eppingwell I'd go.

LORAINE

(Jealously.) Mrs. Eppingwell!

VANDERLIP

Of course, but it's all right, Loraine. She don't count.

LORAINE

Of course not. But then, Floyd, I care so much for you that I can't help a little jealousy—but there, there, you must go. Good-by, dear.

VANDERLIP

Good-by dear, dear Loraine. (Turns to go toward left.)

LORAINE

(Softly.) Floyd!

VANDERLIP

(Turns back, waits, and after a pause.) Well?

LORAINE

(With sweet reproof.)

I've been hearing things about you, sir.

VANDERLIP

What's up now?

LORAINE

Oh, you seem to have—how shall I say!—a penchant for foreigners.

VANDERLIP

(Mystified.)

Darned if I know what you're talking about. Penchant—is that something to eat?

LORAINE

(Laughing.)

Well, then, there is a certain woman, supposed to be Greek, at any rate a foreigner like myself; but with the most adorable accent—or so the men say—

VANDERLIP

(Interrupting.)

Freda, you mean.

LORAINE

(Fastidious expression on face.)

Yes, I believe that is the woman's name.

Vanderlip (Laughing jovially.)

There ain't anything in it. I don't care a rap for her—not a rap.

LORAINE

Then there's that Mrs. Eppingwell. I can't help thinking you are a little devoted to her.

VANDERLIP

(Showing slight embarrassment.)

Oh, well, I've only seen her in a social way—that's all, in a social way.

LORAINE

And you do love only me?

(He nods.)

Then tell me that you do.

23

VANDERLIP

(With impulsive eagerness, half lifting his arms as if to embrace her and controlling himself with an effort.)

Oh, I do, Loraine. I do, I do.

LORAINE

It is sweet to hear you say it. And now you really must go. Good-by, dear, good-by.

(He crosses stage to left and goes out.)

(She starts to cross stage to rear, but is approached and stopped by Sitka Charley.)

SITKA CHARLEY

(Gruffly.) Good morning.

LORAINE

(Sweetly.)

Good morning, Charley.

SITKA CHARLEY

(Bluntly.)

You got my money?

LORAINE

Oh, let me see. How much is it?

SITKA CHARLEY

Two hundred dollar.

LORAINE

I'll tell you. You come to my cabin to-morrow morning, and I'll give it to you.

SITKA CHARLEY

(Not letting on that he knows she is lying.) To-morrow morning you give me money?

LORAINE

At my cabin, don't forget.

SITKA CHARLEY

All right, to-morrow morning.

(He turns abruptly and starts to go toward stove.)

LORAINE

(Calling.)

Oh, Charley!

(He turns back to her.)

Is Dominion Creek very rich?

SITKA CHARLEY

Dam rich.

LORAINE

And do you know whether Mr. Vanderlip has any claims there?

SITKA CHARLEY

Me no know.

(Starts to go.)

LORAINE

(Detaining him.)

But Mr. Vanderlip is very rich, isn't he? You know that?

SITKA CHARLEY

Vanderlip dam rich.

(Sitka Charley turns abruptly and goes back to stove.)

(Loraine crosses stage to left rear to counter, where a clerk waits upon her.)

(Enter Mrs. Eppingwell and Mrs. McFee from right. Both engage in brushing snow from moccasins.)

MRS. EPPINGWELL

(Finishing first, and looking about the store as if in quest of some one.) as I don't see anything of Captain Eppingwell, and he is the soul of promptness.

MRS. McFEE

(Still brushing snow.)

Mayhap we are a bit early, Mrs. Eppingwell. But as I was saying, it's verra dootful morals the giving of this masked ball. Masked, mind you, with every low dance-hall creature a-dying to come and put decent folk to the shame of their company. I speak my mind, and it's ay shameful that honest bodies must be so sore put. There'll be ruffians and gamblers with masks over their sinful faces, and who's to know? And there's that Freda woman. 'Tis said she plays with the souls of men as a child with a wee bit of a pipe plays with soap-bubbles. And there's all the rest—bold hussies!—who's to stop them from flaunting their fine feathers in our faces? Who's to stop them, I make free to ask?

MRS. EPPINGWELL

(Smiling.)

The doorkeeper, of course. It is quite simple. Masks must be lifted at the door.

MRS. McFEE

Ou, ay, verra simple, I should say. Belike you'll undertake the doorkeeping, and belike you'll know the face of every rapscallion of them.

MRS. EPPINGWELL

We'll get one of the men who do know—Mr. Prince, for example. There he is, by the stove. We'll ask him to be doorkeeper.

(Prince goes to rear and joins Loraine.)

MRS. McFEE

(With more than usual asperity.)

And how comes it Mr. Prince should know the children of sin and still be company for decent bodies?

MRS. EPPINGWELL

Because he is a man, I imagine.

(Mrs. McFee snorts.)

There is Sitka Charley. I suppose you would bar him if he wanted to come?

MRS. MCFEE

(Judicially.)

Why, no, he's a verra good soul.

MRS. EPPINGWELL

Yet I'm sure he knows all the children of sin, you call them.

MRS. McFEE

But he's an Indian, and he doesna dance.

MRS. EPPINGWELL

(Laughing.)

Then I suppose I shall not shock you by speaking to him.

(Approaches Sitka Charley, while Mrs. McFee goes to counter and is waited on by a clerk.)

Good morning, Charley. Have you seen Captain Eppingwell?

SITKA CHARLEY

(Nodding good morning.)

Yes.

Mrs. Eppingwell How long ago? Was he here?

SITKA CHARLEY

I see um last night.

MRS. EPPINGWELL

Oh!

(Laughing.)

I've seen him later than that. But he was to meet me here.

SITKA CHARLEY

Um.

MRS. EPPINGWELL

(Trying to make conversation.)

It is rather cold this morning.

Um.

SITKA CHARLEY

MRS. EPPINGWELL

How cold?

SITKA CHARLEY

Sixty-five below. Any dogs to sell?

MRS. EPPINGWELL

Still trying to buy dogs! For whom this time? Sitka Charley

Vanderlip. He want eight dogs.

MRS. EPPINGWELL

(Startled and interested.) Mr. Vanderlip?

Um.

SITKA CHARLEY

Mrs. Eppingwell What does he want with dogs?

Sitka Charley Um. Got dogs?

MRS. EPPINGWELL

(A sudden thought striking her.)

Yes, I've dogs to sell. Or rather, Captain Eppingwell has.

SITKA CHARLEY

Fresh dogs? Strong dogs?

MRS. EPPINGWELL

(Considering.)

Well, no. You see, he just arrived yesterday. It was a long trip.

SITKA CHARLEY

Yes, me know—sixteen hundred miles. Dogs all bones, all played out, no good.

MRS. EPPINGWELL

How soon does he want the dogs?

SITKA CHARLEY

Right away, now, to-day.

MRS. EPPINGWELL

What does he want the dogs for?

SITKA CHARLEY

(Stolidly.)

Um?

MRS. EPPINGWELL

What does Mr. Vanderlip want the dogs for?

SITKA CHARLEY

That no Sitka Charley's business. That Vanderlip's business.

MRS. EPPINGWELL

But I want to know.

SITKA CHARLEY

Then you ask Vanderlip.

MRS. EPPINGWELL

Tell me.

SITKA CHARLEY

Much better you ask Vanderlip, I think so.

(A pause, during which Sitka Charley merely waits, while Mrs. Eppingwell seems to be thinking. When she speaks, it is in a changed, serious tone.)

MRS. EPPINGWELL

Charley, we have travelled the Long Trail together, you and I.

SITKA CHARLEY

Um.

MRS. EPPINGWELL

We journeyed through the Hills of Silence. We saw our last dogs drop in the traces. We staggered and fell, and crawled on our hands and knees through the snow because we had not enough to eat, and it was very cold. We had our last food stolen—

SITKA CHARLEY

(Eyes flashing, face stiffening, grimly and with satisfaction.)

Captain Eppingwell kill one man who steal food. I kill other man. I know.

MRS. EPPINGWELL

(Shuddering.)

Yes, it was terrible. But we kept the faith of food and blanket, you and I, Charley.

SITKA CHARLEY

And Captain Eppingwell.

MRS. EPPINGWELL

And Captain Eppingwell. And by that faith of food and blanket I want you to tell me the truth now.

SITKA CHARLEY

Um.

MRS. EPPINGWELL

(Eagerly.)

Will you?

SITKA CHARLEY

(Nodding his head.)

Um.

MRS. EPPINGWELL

(Hurriedly.)

Mr. Vanderlip wants dogs, fresh dogs—why? Sitka Charley

He make a long travel, many sleeps.

Mrs. Eppingwell Where? When? Tell me all.

SITKA CHARLEY

Um travel down river. Um start to-night.

Mrs. Eppingwell He goes alone?

SITKA CHARLEY

(Shaking his head.)

No.

MRS. EPPINGWELL

Who goes with him?

Me go.

SITKA CHARLEY

MRS. EPPINGWELL

(Irritably.)

Yes, yes, of course. But you don't count. Anybody else?

SITKA CHARLEY

(Nodding his head.)

Um.

MRS. EPPINGWELL

(Triumphantly.)

Just as I thought. Tell me, Charley, it is—it is this—er—this horrid woman? You know.

SITKA CHARLEY

Um, this bad woman—this damn bad woman. Um, she go with him, to-night, twelve o'clock, the water-hole. She meet um there.

Mrs. Eppingwell (Eagerly.)

Yes, yes. And then....

SITKA CHARLEY

And then she go with um, many sleeps, down the river.

MRS. EPPINGWELL

And you will get the dogs?

SITKA CHARLEY

Sure, I get um.

(Enter Dave Harney from left, striding angrily.) I get um now—

DAVE HARNEY

Good-by.

(Starts in the direction of Dave Harney.)

MRS. EPPINGWELL

Wait a minute, Charley.

SITKA CHARLEY

(Over his shoulder.)

I come back. You wait.

(Approaches Dave Harney.)

Hello, Dave. Cold to-day.

DAVE HARNEY

(Whirling upon him savagely.)

You betcher life it's cold—regular freeze-out, with me frozen. But I'm goin' to quit it, quit it cold. I'll harness up my dogs and hit the high places for a land of justice where a man can get what he's ordered a year before and paid for.

SITKA CHARLEY

Got any dogs to sell?

DAVE HARNEY

Got any sugar to sell?

SITKA CHARLEY

I buy um dogs.

DAVE HARNEY

I'm buyin' sugar.

SITKA CHARLEY

I got no sugar. You got dogs. I buy dogs eight dogs—how much?

Dave Harney Five hundred dollars a dog.

SITKA CHARLEY

Um—eight dogs—four thousand dollar.

DAVE HARNEY

Dogs is wuth what you're willin' to pay for 'em.

SITKA CHARLEY

Um.

DAVE HARNEY

Look here, Charley, I used to be a miner, but I'm a business man now. Got any sugar?

SITKA CHARLEY

No sugar.

DAVE HARNEY

I'll throw a lot off them dogs for some sugar. No sugar, they cost you four thousand.

(Turns to go.)

SITKA CHARLEY

(Making no movement to detain him.)

Um.

DAVE HARNEY

(Over his shoulder.)

Four thousand,

CHARLEY

Um.

SITKA CHARLEY

They're wuth it if you want 'em real bad.

SITKA CHARLEY

All right, Dave. I buy.

DAVE HARNEY

Bring the dust around to my cabin at one o'clock.

SITKA CHARLEY

I buy now.

DAVE HARNEY

No, you don't. I'm goin' back to tell 'em what I think of 'em, the skunks! They've got sweetenin' in plenty for their own mush and coffee. You betcher life they have, and I'm goin' to get some of it or know the reason why.

(Storms out through door to lejt.)

(Sitka Charley returns to Mrs. Eppingwell.)

SITKA CHARLEY

That Dave Harney all the same one big robber. But I get um dogs all right.

MRS. EPPINGWELL

Tell me about this—er—this woman, Charley, this Freda—Freda Moloof her name is, isn't it?

SITKA CHARLEY

(Showing plainly that his attention has been called off from the consideration of Loraine Lisznayi.)

Oh, Freda!

MRS. EPPINGWELL

(Smiling.)

You call her Freda.

SITKA CHARLEY

Everybody call her Freda. Um good name. Me like it.

MRS. EPPINGWELL

Well, what kind of a woman is she?

SITKA CHARLEY

Um good woman.

MRS. EPPINGWELL

(With an angry movement of arm and clenching of hand.)

Oh!

SITKA CHARLEY

(Looking surprised and getting stubborn.) Me know Freda long time—two years. Um good woman. Um tongue speak true. Um just like you, no afraid. Um just like you, travel Long Trail with me. No afraid, very soft heart; sorry for dogs; no ride on sled when dogs tired. Um tired, but um walk. And um tongue straight; all the time speak true. I am Sitka Charley—I know.

MRS. EPPINGWELL

Yes, yes. Go on.

SITKA CHARLEY

(Considering.)

Freda no like men.

MRS. EPPINGWELL

Now that is too much, Charley? How about Mr. Vanderlip?

SITKA CHARLEY

(Shrugs his shoulders.)

I know Freda long time. Freda know Vanderlip short time. Maybe Freda like Vanderlip. I don't know. But before she never like men, that I know. Maybe you like Mr. Vanderlip I think. (Mrs. Eppingwell smiles, and Sitka Charley grows more positive.) Vanderlip come your cabin all the time. You ride on Vanderlip's sled. I know. I see. Maybe you like Vanderlip.

MRS. EPPINGWELL

You don't understand, Charley. I have reasons for being nice to Mr.

Vanderlip.

SITKA CHARLEY

(Sceptically.)

Um.

MRS. EPPINGWELL

And, Charley, you mustn't tell anybody what you have told me about Mr. Vanderlip going away to-night with that—that woman.

SITKA CHARLEY

(Weighing her words.)

Maybe I tell Freda.

MRS. EPPINGWELL

(Stamping foot angrily.)

Don't be foolish, Charley. She is the last person in the world who ought to know. Of course you'll not tell her. Tell no one.

(Sitka Charley hesitates.)

Promise me you'll not tell. Promise me by the faith of food and blanket.

SITKA CHARLEY

(Reluctantly.)

All right, I no tell.

MRS. EPPINGWELL

They say Freda is a dancer. Have you seen her dance?

SITKA CHARLEY

(Nodding his heady a pleased expression on his face.)

I see um. Very good dance. Um dance at Juneau, two years ago, first time I see. Treadwell Mine no work that day. No men to work. All men come Juneau and look see Freda dance. Freda makum much money. Um speak to me. Um say, "Charley, I go Yukon Country. You drive my dogs, how much?" Then Freda travel Long Trail with me.

MRS. EPPINGWELL

They say many men like her.

SITKA CHARLEY

(Nodding head vigorously.)

Um, sure. Me like her too, very much.

MRS. EPPINGWELL

(Smiling tolerantly.)

And they say she makes fools of men.

SITKA CHARLEY

Sure. Dam fools. Men just like bubble. Freda just make play with um—smash!—just like that. Everybody say so.

MRS. EPPINGWELL

What kind of a looking woman is she?

SITKA CHARLEY

You no see um?

Mrs. Eppingwell No. What does she look like?

(Freda enters from right.)

SITKA CHARLEY

(Looking at Freda.)

Um there now.

MRS. EPPINGWELL

(Not understanding.)

What?

SITKA CHARLEY

(Nodding head toward Freda.)

Um Freda there.

(Mrs. Eppingwell turns involuntarily to look. Freda pauses on entering, starts as though to retreat at sight of the crowd, then stiffens herself, face and body, to meet it, and proceeds to brush snow from moccasins. There is silence in store. Then a perturbation amongst miners about stove, men craning their heads over one another's shoulders to look at Freda. The clerks look at her. Everybody looks at her.)

(Mrs. McFee turns up her nose several degrees, and, plainly advertising a highly moral rage, walks over to Mrs. Eppingwell.)

MRS. McFEE

(To Mrs. Eppingwell, but glaring at Freda.)

It's my way of thinking that it is high time for decent bodies to be going.

(Sitka Charley glares angrily at Mrs. McFee.)

MRS. EPPINGWELL

(In low voice.)

Hush. It is a public place, and she has as much right here as you or I. Don't insult the poor woman.

MRS. McFEE

(Snorting.)

In my way of thinking the insult's the other way around. Come you, Mrs. Eppingwell, we must go. The verra air is contameenated.

MRS. EPPINGWELL

(Pleadingly.)

Do please restrain yourself, Mrs. McFee. Don't make a scene.

MRS. MCFEE

(Raising her voice.)

I'll no restrain myself, and I'll no wait for you if you see proper no to come now. The hussy!

(Mrs. McFee, nose high in the air, turns to make exit at right. Freda has just finished brushing snow, and has risen erect. Mrs. McFee, passing her to go out the door, sniffs audibly and draws aside her skirt. Freda makes no movement, though her lips tighten. Exit Mrs. McFee. Freda tries to hang up wisp-broom, but her hand trembles, misses peg, and wisp-broom falls to floor. She picks it up and this time hangs it properly. Turns and goes to right rear to counter, where clerk waits upon her.)

SITKA CHARLEY

(Glaring after Mrs. McFee, angrily).

That womans no like Freda. What for?

MRS. EPPINGWELL

(Speaking gently.)

No women like Freda.

SITKA CHARLEY

(Stunned, slowly.)

You no like Freda?

MRS. EPPINGWELL

(More gently even than before.)

No, Charley, I do not like Freda.

SITKA CHARLEY

(Showing anger.)

What for you no like Freda?

MRS. EPPINGWELL

I cannot explain. You would not understand.

SITKA CHARLEY

(More anger.)

Me Sitka Charley. Me understand. What for you no like Freda?

(Captain Eppingwell enters from right.)

MRS. EPPINGWELL

I—

(Catching sight of Capt. Eppingwell.) There is Captain Eppingwell now.

(Capt. Eppingwell brushes moccasins quickly, and goes immediately to Mrs. Eppingwell. Sitka Charley, still angry, joins group about stove.)

CAPT. EPPINGWELL

Early, as usual, Maud.

MRS. EPPINGWELL

No, merely on time. It is you who are late. Capt. Eppingwell

Impossible!

(Looks at his watch and smiles triumphantly.)

I knew it. On time to the tick of the second.

MRS. EPPINGWELL

(Smiling.)

Not by Dawson time.

CAPT. EPPINGWELL

Oh! of course. I haven't changed my watch. I'm still going by sun-time. Sorry.

MRS. EPPINGWELL

(Smiling.)

I forgive you. It is the first time, but I really can't count it against you.

CAPT. EPPINGWELL

(Looking closely into her face.)

What's wrong?

MRS. EPPINGWELL

Archie, you're the dearest man I know. Of course there is something wrong, and of course you knew it as soon as you set eyes on me. Well, I am beaten.

CAPT. EPPINGWELL

The Ever-Victorious-One beaten! Impossible! I'll not believe it.

MRS. EPPINGWELL

I am, just the same. Here I have been trying to save Floyd Vanderlip, counteracting that evil woman's influence, having him to tea and dinner and giving him no end of my time, and Flossie isn't here yet, and he runs away with Freda Mo-loof to-night. It's all arranged, and everything.

CAPT. EPPINGWELL

But—but—wait a minute. Enlighten me. I am only a poor traveller. Who is this Flossie? And why shouldn't this Vanderlip-man—whoever he is—run away if he wants to?

MRS. EPPINGWELL

How ridiculous of me! I forget you've been away. You know who Freda Moloof is?

CAPT. EPPINGWELL

Surely, surely. She has the most magnificent furs and the most magnificent dogs in all Alaska. A fascinating creature, I—er—understand. She plays with men as a child plays with bubbles.

MRS. EPPINGWELL

It seems to me I've heard that before.

CAPT. EPPINGWELL

It has become a saying in the country.

MRS. EPPINGWELL

I have heard of men who whistle women up as they would whistle dogs. She must be the type of woman that whistles men.

CAPT. EPPINGWELL

(Warmly.)

All she has to do is look at a man.

MRS. EPPINGWELL

(Smiling.)

You speak as though she had looked at you.

CAPT. EPPINGWELL

(Smiling.)

A very interesting woman.

MRS. EPPINGWELL

Well, anyway, she has cast eyes and wiles upon Floyd Vanderlip.

CAPT. EPPINGWELL

But why shouldn't she? This is a free country.

MRS. EPPINGWELL

Wait a minute. I'm trying to explain. Floyd Vanderlip is engaged to marry some one else.

CAPT. EPPINGWELL

O-o-h!

MRS. EPPINGWELL

Floyd Vanderlip is a big, strong man. For five years he chased Eldorados over the ice-fields, living on moose and salmon and working like a beast. He never had an idle moment in which to be wicked. Then he struck it on Klondike and is worth millions and millions. Also, he sat down for the first time in five years and rested.

He remembered a girl who was waiting for him down in the States—a young thing—and sent for her to come in. They were to be married as soon as she arrived. He has a cabin all ready. Well, that's Flossie. She is coming in over the ice now—he's told me all about it—and ought to be here any day. I've been looking for her, and looking for her, till I am almost sick. Then this Freda Moloof cast her spell upon him. I heard the gossip—

CAPT. EPPINGWELL

And proceeded to take a hand. I begin to understand.

MRS. EPPINGWELL

I did my best to break her influence. The time and thought I've wasted upon that man! It's almost scandalous the way I've devoted myself to him! Sitka Charley believes I am in love with him—told me so to my face. And it's all wasted, card parties and everything. What was I against the only woman in Klondike who possesses a piano and a maid? And to-night he runs away down the river with her.

CAPT. EPPINGWELL

With Freda Moloof?

MRS. EPPINGWELL

With Freda Moloof. There she is now, buying things for the journey most probably.

CAPT. EPPINGWELL

(Turning to look at Freda, and turning back again.)

I must say she couldn't have done better if he is worth all you say he is. I remember him now, a strapping fellow, brave as a lion and all that.

MRS. EPPINGWELL

Yes, but he's caressed more shovel-handles than women's hands, and that's the trouble with him. And I don't know what I shall do.

CAPT. EPPINGWELL

You could scarcely serve an injunction on him.

MRS. EPPINGWELL

I don't know what I'll do. Floyd Vanderlip is not the sort of man to appeal to. To try to impress him to do the right thing would be like setting fire to a powder mill. I wish I knew how near Flossie is. There hasn't been a courier or a mail carrier in for weeks and weeks. The mail from Dyea is twenty days overdue.

(Enter Mail Carrier, carrying leather mail-pouch. He is clad in a long squirrel-skin parka reaching to his knees, the hood drawn over his head and ears and leaving only jace exposed. Face and mouth are iced-up, making speech impossible. He does not stop to brush snow jrom moccasins, but proceeds rapidly to cross to stove.)

CAPT. EPPINGWELL

There is the man who can tell you about Flossie. Shall I ask him?

MRS. EPPINGWELL

Oh! the mail carrier? At last! And in the nick of time. Yes, do.

CAPT. EPPINGWELL

(Stepping into the path of the Mail Carrier.)

What's the news?

(Mail Carrier makes dumb show that he cannot speak, waving his arms and pointing to his iced mouth and then to the stove.)

(Capt. Eppingwell laughs and lets him pass.)

(To Mrs. Eppingwell.)

He's so iced up he cannot speak. Wait till he thaws out, and then I'll get hold of him. In the meantime—

MRS. EPPINGWELL

(Interrupting.)

In the meantime you must meet the Lisznayi.

CAPT. EPPINGWELL

The Lisznayi!

MRS. EPPINGWELL

Yes, she is a fascinating woman, our latest acquisition. An Old World Hungarian with all the do and dare of the New World blood. She was a friend of the Queen of Roumania. Posed as a model for the Queen. Had cardinals and princes at her beck and call. Plenty of money, of course, position, and all that. Came into the Klondike out of sheer love of adventure, and possibly because she was bored. You'll enjoy her, I know. There she is over there. Do you care to?

(Mrs. Eppingwell and Capt. Eppingwell walk over to left rear to Loraine Lisznayi and Prince.)

(Mail Carrier tries to get to stove, but is blocked by miners, who are demanding: "What's the news?" "How's the trail?" "Any letters for me?" "And me?" "And me?" "Where did you meet O'Brien? He left ten days ago." "How's

47

the ice on Thirty Mile River?" etc.y etc. To all of which Mail Carrier replies by waving his arms and thrusting through the crowd till he gets to stove, over which he holds his Face.)

(Dave Harney enters from left, still in towering rage, but his jace lights up, as though struck by a sudden thought when he catches sight oj Mail Carrier. He strides over, clutches Mail Carrier by the arm and draws him to one side.)

DAVE HARNEY

(In a whisper.)

Got a noospaper?

MAIL CARRIER

(Nods head.)

DAVE HARNEY

How many?

MAIL CARRIER

(Holds up one finger.)

DAVE HARNEY

I'll give you twenty dollars for it.

MAIL CARRIER

(Shakes head.)

DAVE HARNEY

(Bidding rapidly, each bid being met by a shake of Mail Carrier's head.) Twenty-five. Thirty. Thirty-five. Forty. Fifty.

MAIL CARRIER

(Nods head and goes back to stove.)

(Freda walks forward toward stove and beckons to Sitka Charley, who leaves group about stove and comes to her.)

FREDA

Tell the Mail Carrier I want to speak to him, Charley.

SITKA CHARLEY

(Obediently.)

Urn.

(Sitka Charley crosses to stove, where Mail Carrier is pulling the ice from his mouth.)

Freda want talk some with you.

MAIL CARRIER

(Turning to look at Freda, nods head and mumbles incoherently, at same time starting to go to Freda and still pulling ice jrom mouth. He shakes hands with Freda and speaks thickly at first.)

How do do, Freda.

FREDA

How do you do, Joe. What kind of a trip did you have?

MAIL CARRIER

Pretty rough, but I made good time just the same. Passed everything in sight.

FREDA

That is what I wanted to ask you about. Did you pass the outfit of a girl, or, rather, of a young woman?

MAIL CARRIER

Coming in by herself, with a dog-puncher and an Indian?

FREDA

Yes. Where did you pass her?

MAIL CARRIER

Yesterday afternoon, about three o'clock. They were making camp early. She was pretty tired from the looks of her.

FREDA

When should she get in?

MAIL CARRIER

I talked with the dog-puncher. He said they'd camp to-night at Mooseback and come in tomorrow. That's twenty-five miles, and if they don't start too late, they'll make Dawson by the middle of the day.

FREDA

What kind of a girl is she?

MAIL CARRIER

Good. How do you mean?

FREDA

I mean what kind of a looking girl is she? How did she strike you?

MAIL CARRIER

Oh, one of the soft and clingy kind, I guess I'd call her. You know, the kind that needs lots of cuddling and petting. Pretty, yes, danged pretty. Blue eyes, wavy hair, and all the rest—trembly lips and teary eyes—smily and weepy, you know, all in the same moment. But, gee! Freda, I can't stand here gassin' all day. I got about a thousand dollars' worth of letters to deliver—a dollar apiece and cheap at the price. I'll see you later. So long.

FREDA

All right, Joe. Tell Sitka Charley I want to see him, will you?

(Mail Carrier returns to stove, picks up mail pouch, and sends Sitka Charley to Freda.)

(Capt. Eppingwell comes to Mail Carrier, and is leading him off to Mrs. Eppingwell when Dave Harney interposes.)

DAVE HARNEY

Hold your hosses, Joe. How about that dicker for the noospaper? You said Yes to fifty.

MAIL CARRIER

(Pulling out his gold sack and drawing newspaper from pocket and giving both to Dave Harney.)

All right. Just weigh the fifty into that.

(Dave Harney takes gold sack over to scales, produces his own gold sack, and a clerk weighs from one sack into the other.)

(Mail Carrier accompanies Capt. Eppingwell to Mrs. Eppingwell.)

(Capt. Eppingwell, Loraine Lisznayi, and Prince move along counter toward right and inspect mittens and moccasins.)

FREDA

What time to-morrow has he decided upon starting?

SITKA CHARLEY

No to-morrow. To-day, to-night, twelve o'clock to-night.

FREDA

(Startled.)

To-night! Are you sure?

Um.

SITKA CHARLEY

FREDA

You said to-morrow.

SITKA CHARLEY

Vanderlip um change mind. Look like much hurry.

FREDA

And the Lisznayi woman?

SITKA CHARLEY

She wait water-hole. Um meet her there. One Indian drive her dogs. Me drive Vanderlip's dogs.

FREDA

But Vanderlip mustn't go to-night.

Charley, he simply mustn't.

I tell you,

SITKA CHARLEY

(Incredulously.)

Um.

FREDA

Not only that, but you must help me to keep him from going.

SITKA CHARLEY

(Angrily.)

What for, Freda? I am Sitka Charley. I buy dogs, I sell dogs, I drive dogs. I help you dogs, yes. What for I help you other things? Vanderlip all the same one big chief. Um womans like um.

(Holding up fingers.)

One, two, three womans like um. That um womans' trouble. No Sitka Charley's trouble. What for, Freda?

FREDA

Why, what are you thinking about?

Sitka Charley I think you one big fool, Freda.

FREDA

(Smiling sadly.)

And I think you are right, Charley, when I look back.

SITKA CHARLEY

No look back. Right now. What for you make fool with Vanderlip? Him no good. Him big fool too.

FREDA

Oh, I see. You think I am in love with him.

Sitka Charley (With satisfaction.)

Um.

FREDA

You really think so?

SITKA CHARLEY

Um. What for you say he must no go to-night? Um?

FREDA

Listen, Charley. You must help me, and I'll tell you all about it. There is a little girl coming in over the ice to marry Vanderlip—

SITKA CHARLEY

(Interrupting excitedly.)

One more woman! Um Vanderlip one dam big chief.

(Holding up fingers.)

One woman, two woman, three woman, four womans.

FREDA

(Surprised.) Four women?

SITKA CHARLEY

Um. Four womans.

FREDA

Who are they?

SITKA CHARLEY

(Holding up fingers.)

Little girl come in over ice—one. Lisznayi woman go 'way with um—two. Freda no want Lisznayi woman go 'way with um—three. Mrs. Eppingwell—four. One—two—three—four—womans.

FREDA

(Surprised.)

Mrs. Eppingwell! Oh, you told me about her once. She was the woman who was with you on that trip through the Hills of Silence. She is a very brave woman. I have heard much of her, and I like her. If I were a man, I could love her. She must be very good, and sweet, and kind.

SITKA CHARLEY

Sure. And um hard like iron sometimes. But um no like you. Um say so. What for um no like you?

FREDA

(Gently.)

No woman likes me, Charley.

SITKA CHARLEY

All men like you.

FREDA

(With touch of anger.)

All men are fools.

SITKA CHARLEY

What for womans no like you?

FREDA

(Meditatively).

And she likes Vanderlip. How do you know? What do you know?

SITKA CHARLEY

No can tell. I promise.

FREDA

Promised whom?

SITKA CHARLEY

Mrs. Eppingwell. Um Mrs. Eppingwell very good woman.

FREDA

But she has a husband. It is not good for her to like another man. What do you think?

SITKA CHARLEY

(Perplexedly.)

I think I don't know. I think all um womans crazy. What for all um womans like this Vanderlip man?

55

FREDA

(Decisively.)

Well, I don't.

SITKA CHARLEY

(Sceptically.)

Um.

FREDA

Let me show you, Charley, and then you will know why I want you to help me. And, remember, you mustn't tell a word of any of this to any one.

SITKA CHARLEY

(Debating the proposition.)

Um—maybe I tell Mrs. Eppingwell.

FREDA

(Angrily.)

Don't be silly, Charley. You mustn't tell anybody. Promise me now.

SITKA CHARLEY

(With despairing perplexity.) All right, I no tell.

FREDA

Now this little girl is coming in over the ice—her name is Flossie. She has lived a soft life down in California, where the sun is warm and there is no snow. She does not know hardship, nor the trail, and she is having a hard time now on the trail. Think of it!—sixty-five degrees below zero this morning, and she is out in it, walking, walking, walking, her breath freezing, her mouth icing up, her eyebrows rimed with frost. And she is very stiff, and sore, and tired. Every step of the trail she takes in pain. It is like a bad dream to her, Charley. But she sees, always before her, at the end of the dream, an awakening at Dawson, in the arms of the man who is to marry her. But, Charley, what if when she gets to Dawson there is no Floyd Vanderlip? no man to marry her? It will break her heart. It will be no happy awakening from a bad dream, but the beginning of a worse dream. And she is a little girl, Charley—not a strong woman like me who does not care. She will care, and she will know nobody, and she will cry, and cry, and cry. Did you ever hear a woman cry, Charley? Think of it, she is only a little girl.

SITKA CHARLEY

Um. More like baby.

FREDA

Yes, put it that way, more like a baby. She cannot stand pain.

SITKA CHARLEY

Oh, on trail, too much walk make um hurt.

FREDA

No, no.

(Holds hand to heart.)

Pain here.

SITKA CHARLEY

Um. I know. Um sick. What um call heart disease. I see one man sick that way. Um fall down dead, just like that.

FREDA

(Irritably.)

Oh, you don't understand.

SITKA CHARLEY

(Puzzled.)

I don't know. Womans all crazy.

FREDA

(Smiling.)

I think I can explain. Last summer you were in a canoe race on the river. You paddled very hard, but you lost.

(Putting hand to heart.)

And it hurt you—

SITKA CHARLEY

(Interrupting.)

Um. Um. Paddle like hell. No win race. (Stroking first one arm and then the other.) Much tired right here.

(Putting hand over heart.)

And um much hurt right here, no tired, just hurt like rheumatism, because I am sorry I lose race.

(Nods head repeatedly.)

Um. Um.

FREDA

The very thing. She doesn't know it, but she is racing against this Lisznayi woman. Flossie must get here before the other woman steals her man. And you must help her win the race. Will you?

SITKA CHARLEY

You know this Flossie girl?

FREDA

No.

SITKA CHARLEY

No?

FREDA

Never saw her in my life. But she is coming into a strange country without a friend or a dollar when she gets here. She will have great trouble. And you know, Charley, it is not good for a woman to be without friends or money in this country.

SITKA CHARLEY

(Puzzled as much as ever.)

Don't know Flossie girl. No like Vanderlip man. What for you care?... Much foolishness. All womans crazy.... All right, I help.

(Mail Carrier has-finished interview with Mrs. Eppingwell, received gold sack back from Dave Harney, and gone out with mail pouch to left. Capt. Eppingwell and Loraine Lisznayi have rejoined Mrs. Eppingwell.)

(Loraine Lisznayi says good-by to them, and starts to make exit to right, passing close to Freda and Sitka Charley. She pauses one or two paces away.)

LORAINE

(Favoring Freda with a quick but sweeping, scornful glance.)

Come here, Charley. I want to speak to you a moment.

(Her conduct angers Sitka Charley, who grows stolid and refuses to move or reply.)

FREDA

Speak with her, Charley.

SITKA CHARLEY

(Sullenly.)

No speak.

(Loraine Lisznayi, scornful expression on face, proceeds on her way, and makes exit to right.)

FREDA

Why didn't you, Charley?

SITKA CHARLEY

(Angrily.)

What for she look at you that way?

FREDA

(Ignoring the question.)

They say she is a rich woman in her own country. But I don't believe it. I think she is after Vanderlip's money.

SITKA CHARLEY

Lisznayi woman no got money. I know. I sell her dogs—eight hundred dollars. She pay me three hundred. Two weeks, three weeks, I no get other five hundred dollars. Um no got five hundred. I say, "My dogs, give me back." She give back. Me have fur robe. Good fur robe. She buy, two hundred dollar. Um no pay. Um have good fur robe. Me no have nothing. Um have cabin. Um no pay rent to Johnson. Um smile very nice, um Johnson wait. I know, I see. Um dogs she got now, Vanderlip give, make present. Um no pay firewood. Um no pay many things.

FREDA

I thought so. And now to win the race. Dogs first of all. Flossie must be brought in to-night. I want you here in Dawson, Charley. So you must send some Indian up the trail with a fresh team of dogs. Flossie camps at Mooseback tonight. He is to let her think that Vanderlip has sent the dogs, and that Vanderlip wants her to come right on to-night. Understand?

SITKA CHARLEY

Um. Sure.

FREDA

(Preparing to start toward door at right.)

Start the dogs right away with a man you can trust. And he must be sure to let Flossie think that Vanderlip sent him. At the best, Flossie can't arrive until late to-night. And there may be delays. You keep on Vanderlip's trail so that you will know always where he is.

(Freda and Sitka Charley start to walk toward the door at right.)

When I send for him you must bring him to me, and I'll hold him till Flossie gets in.

SITKA CHARLEY

(Touching Freda's arm.)

No very strong, Freda.

FREDA

(Tapping her forehead.)

Vanderlip no very strong, Charley.

(Both cover ears, pull on mittens, and go out.)

(Dave Harney, unobserved, has been squatting on hams in front of counter to right, intently reading newspaper. He is making dumb show of excited interest. One of the miners discovers him, runs over to him, and starts to read newspaper over his shoulder. Dave Harney folds newspaper across, resting it on his knee, and looks up coolly into face of Miner.)

MINER

(In hurt voice.)

Can't you give a fellow a squint at your paper?

DAVE HARNEY

Got any sugar?

Sure.

MINER

DAVE HARNEY

Give me a whack at your sugar barrel?

MINER

(Surprised and shocked.)

No.

DAVE HARNEY

Then nary squint at my noospaper.

(In meantime other miners and clerks have surrounded him, all demanding to see his newspaper. Whereupon he puts paper in his pocket, rises to his feet, and starts toward door to right, miners and clerks following him and grumbling at his meanness.)

DAVE HARNEY

(Pausing with his hand on door.)

You think you're smart, don't you? Got a corner on sugar, eh? And poor Dave Harney left without no sweetenin' for his coffee an' mush. Well, poor Dave Harney's got a corner on noos. When you want noos, come an' see him, an' be sure an bring your sugar along.

(Goes out, followed by miners.)

(Mrs. Eppingwell and Capt. Eppingwell come forward to stove and warm their hands.)

CAPT. EPPINGWELL

(Continuing conversation.)

Perhaps Freda doesn't know about Flossie. I always thought her a good girl at heart.

MRS. EPPINGWELL

Why this haste then? Why are they running away to-night instead of to-morrow as they had planned? They must have received information somehow, even before the mail carrier arrived. (Enter Mail Carrier from left.)

And look how she captured the mail carrier at once, and for one thing, I know, to learn Flossie's whereabouts.

CAPT. EPPINGWELL

Here he is now. Let's ask him.

(Beckons Mail Carrier over to him.)

You were talking with Freda a little while ago. What did she want to learn?

MAIL CARRIER

(Pausing only long enough to reply, and then going on to make exit to right.) Same thing as your wife—where I passed that girl's outfit.

MRS. EPPINGWELL

(Quietly.)

I knew it.

CAPT. EPPINGWELL

But why couldn't I go around, or you, and talk with Freda, explain the situation fully to her, and make an appeal to whatever good is in her?

Mrs. Eppingwell (Smiling.)

You don't know women, Archie,

(Adding as an afterthought.)

Well as women know women. No, she must be beaten at her own game. Flossie must arrive before midnight to-night.

CAPT. EPPINGWELL

But she camps at Mooseback.

MRS. EPPINGWELL

There are dogs in Dawson. Now, Archie, this is for you to do. Borrow a team of fresh dogs somewhere, put your Indian in charge of it, that one-eyed man, he's faithful, and start him up the trail to Flossie. Let her think Floyd Vanderlip has sent the dogs to bring her in right away.

CAPT. EPPINGWELL

(Smiling.)

Ah, I see. The impatience of the ardent and long-denied lover.

MRS. EPPINGWELL

(Smiling in return.)

And once Flossie is here and gets her arms around Floyd Vanderlip's neck, Freda Moloof will wait in vain at the water-hole.

CAPT. EPPINGWELL

That will settle it. Freda's not the woman to stand knocking her feet around a water-hole very long for any man.

MRS. EPPINGWELL

(Good-naturedly.)

You seem to know a great deal about what kind of a woman this dancer is.

CAPT. EPPINGWELL

I know enough about her, when it comes to Vanderlip and Flossie, to think her the best of the boiling... and to have a sneaking regret for her being beaten this way.

MRS. EPPINGWELL

You may be kind-hearted, Archie, but you are unwise.

CAPT. EPPINGWELL

(Sighing.)

Oh, well, after the manner of civilized man I submit to my womenkind. All right, I'll send the dogs at once.

(Makes a movement to start toward door to right, and Mrs. Eppingwell starts with him.)

(Mrs. Eppingwell, struck suddenly by a new idea, pauses. Capt. Eppingwell pauses a step in advance and looks at her.)

What's wrong now?

MRS. EPPINGWELL

Suppose there is some mischance, a delay, and Flossie doesn't get in by midnight?

CAPT. EPPINGWELL

Then Freda wins.

MRS. EPPINGWELL

(Decisively.)

No, she doesn't.

(Thinks for a moment.)

Floyd Vanderlip is coming to the ball. I'll see that he comes. I'll be very nice to him and watch him closely so that he does not sneak away. If Flossie fails to arrive, say by half-past eleven, I'll be taken ill, and I'll ask Vanderlip to take me home; and I'll hold him, no matter how terribly ill or terribly nice I have to be, until midnight is well past or until Flossie arrives.

CAPT. EPPINGWELL

Then it's my duty to disappear about the time you are taken ill.

MRS. EPPINGWELL

Archie, though I tell you for the thousandth time, you are a perfect dear.

65

And I can be as terribly nice as I please to Floyd Vanderlip?

(Capt. Eppingwell laughs and nods, and they continue toward door.)

MRS. EPPINGWELL

(While they are pulling on mittens, etc.)

And now the dogs. Don't delay a moment, Archie, please.

CAPT. EPPINGWELL

The one-eyed man and the six dogs start at once.

(They go out.)

(Only clerks behind counter are left on the stage.)

(Nothing happens for a full minute, when Mrs. McFee appears at right, peeping through door, which she holds ajar. She peers cautiously about, enters, and sniffs the air several times. Then she smiles a sour smile of satisfaction.)

MRS. McFEE

And now a decent body can make her purchases.

CURTAIN

ACT II—ANTEROOM OF PIONEER HALL

Scene. *Anteroom of Pioneer Hall. It is ten-thirty P.M. The room is large and bare. Its walls are of logs, stuffed between with brown moss. Street door to rear, in centre. Doors, window-frames, and sashes of rough, unstained pine boards. At one side of door is wisp-broom for brushing snow from moccasins. On either side of door is an ordinary small-paned window, and beneath either window is a rough wooden bench. Under benches are large out-door moccasins, left there after the manner of overshoes, by their owners. In available space on rear wall, many wooden pegs, on which are hanging furs, parkas, hats, wraps, etc. Midway between front and rear, and at equal distances between centre and sides, running at full blast, are two large wood-burning stoves. Alongside each stove is a wood-box filled with firewood. On right, a window. On left, wide doorway, open, connecting with ballroom. Through doorway come occasional snatches of dance-music, bursts of laughter and of voices. Because it is very cold, street door is kept closed, and is opened by doorkeeper only when some one knocks, and then only long enough for that one to enter. All parleying is done on inside with door closed. Prince, as doorkeeper, is standing at rear by street door. Men and women, in costume, are disappearing through door to left, from where come strains of a waltz.*

PRINCE

(Drawing up his shoulders, as if cold.) B-r-r!

(Crosses rapidly to lejt and peers through doorway into ballroom, looking jor somebody. Holds up his finger and beckons.) Here, you, Billy! More fire! Hi yu skookum fire!

(Enter Indian, who proceeds to fire up both stoves.)

(Prince stands looking into ballroom. A knock is heard at street door. He returns and opens door.)

(A Man enters, masked and in heavy fur overcoat.)

PRINCE

(Hastily closing door.)

Hello.

(The Man hesitates, looks around, and starts to cross to left.)

PRINCE

(Plucking him by the arm.)

Well?

MAN

(Pausing, and then, as if discovering reason for his detention.)

Oh!

(Sits down on bench and proceeds to remove moccasins.)

PRINCE

Masks must be lifted at the door, you know.

MAN

(In muffled voice.)

And give myself away? Oh, no.

PRINCE

The doorkeeper's lips are sealed. I give nobody's identity away. Come on, let's see who you are.

(Reaches out and lifts mask.)

Jack Denison!

MAN

(In clear voice.)

Yours truly, Prince, my boy.

PRINCE

But you can't come in here, old man.

MAN

And why not?

PRINCE

(Stuttering and stammering.)

Why—I—they're damned select—it's the women, you know—and I—they—well, they made me doorkeeper, and—

(Breaking down.)

—you know well enough yourself, Jack.

MAN

(Rising as though to go, and in angry tones.) By God, you can come down to Jack Denison's joint all right, and buck Jack Denison's faro layout all right, and have a social drink with him all right; but when Jack Denison comes up to your doings, you turn'm down like he had smallpox.

PRINCE

It's not my fault. It's the women, I tell you. They're running the show.

MAN

(Wheedlingly.)

You might let a fellow in just for a peep. Nobody'll know. I'll clear out before they unmask.

PRINCE

(Pleadingly.)

I can't really, old man, I—

(Catches sight oj Mrs. McFee, who appears in doorway to left.)

Look at her! Get out quick!

(Places hand on his shoulder in friendly way and starts to shove him out.)

MAN

(Catching sight of Mrs. McFee.)

Wow!

(With bodily expression of fear, shrinks behind Prince and allows himself to be shoved out.)

MRS. McFEE

(Crossing over to Prince, and suspiciously.) Who might that body be?

PRINCE

(Wiping his brow.)

One of the unelect, I am sorry to say, Mrs. McFee.

MRS. McFEE

A gambler man, I take it?

(Prince nods.)

But I can no see, Mr. Prince, why you should conduct negotiations inside the door, contameenating the air with the bodily presence of the children of sin.

PRINCE

(Slight note of anger in his voice.)

Do you know how cold it is, Mrs. McFee?

MRS. MCFEE

I have no given it a thought.

PRINCE

Well, it's seventy degrees below zero, and still going down. If that door is open one minute, a refrigerator would be comfortable alongside that ballroom. And if you don't like the way I'm doing things—

(A knock is heard, and he opens door. Sitka Charley squeezes in.)

PRINCE

(Very politely.)

Can Sitka Charley come in, Mrs. McFee?

MRS. McFEE

(Turning to go.)

He is a good body. There is no reason why he should not bide a wee.

(To Sitka Charley.)

But you must go right away again, Charley.

SITKA CHARLEY

(Nods his head, and then to Prince.) Where um Vanderlip?

PRINCE

He's here somewhere. Go and find him.

(Laughter and voices, and many couples enter from lejt, some in costume, several in hooded dominos.)

SITKA CHARLEY

(Recoiling, startled and excited.)

What that?

(Prince laughs.)

What for? Everybody crazy?

PRINCE

(Laughing.)

Button, button, who's got the button. Go and find him.

(Sitka Charley, walking stealthily, like a wild animal in dangerous territory, goes adventuring amongst the maskers.) (After some time, a domino takes Sitka Charley by the arm and leads him apart.)

SITKA CHARLEY

(Dragging back and struggling to escape.) What for, crazymans?

VANDERLIP

Shut up! It's me, Vanderlip. Looking for me?

SITKA CHARLEY

(With relief.)

Um.

VANDERLIP

Anything wrong?

SITKA CHARLEY

(Shaking head.)

No wrong. All right. Um Freda want you come right away.

VANDERLIP

(Surprised.)

Freda! What's she want with me?

SITKA CHARLEY

Um no tell. Um say: "Charley, you go Pioneer Hall quick. All the same one big dance. You catch um Vanderlip. You make um come right away."

VANDERLIP

(Puzzled.)

Where?

SITKA CHARLEY

Um Freda's cabin. You come now?

VANDERLIP

(Thinks for a minute, with a bothered air.) I'll come in a little while. You tell her.

(Turns to rejoin dancers, and speaks over shoulder.)

Dogs all right?

SITKA CHARLEY

Um.

VANDERLIP

Be at the water-hole at twelve o'clock?

SITKA CHARLEY

Um. Sure.

(Sitka Charley gains street door and goes out.)

(A knock is heard at door. Enter Dave Harney, costumed as a Scotch minister. He passes Prince's inspection, removes street moccasins and parka, and walks to the front. His shambling, loose-jointed gait discovers him. There is hand-clapping and laughter, and there are cries of "Harney! Harney!" "Dave Harney!" Crowd singsy "For the sugar-man will catch you if you don't watch out." He accepts the discovery, goes over to stove at right, pulls newspaper out of pocket, and begins to read. The dancers crowd about him, demanding the news. He makes to be offended by them and walks away, reading paper. They follow behind him, still clamoring for the news. He promenades about stage and then makes exit to left, followed by the whole crew, with the exception of one domino and a Court Lady of the time of Louis XVI, who linger by stove to left.)

COURT LADY

Mrs. Eppingwell I haven't seen your make-up, Archie.

CAPT. EPPINGWELL

Domino,

(In disguised voice, declaiming.)

Would that I might claim Archie for myself, there is such affectionate possession in the way you say it. Who is this Archie, sweet lady?

MRS. EPPINGWELL

Come, come, Archie, a truce to fooling. Besides, you can't fool me anyway. Did you get the dogs off?

CAPT. EPPINGWELL

(In natural voice.)

Promptly, and with the one-eyed man. Also a spare man to come back post-haste and let us know their progress.

MRS. EPPINGWELL

Then when should Flossie arrive?

CAPT. EPPINGWELL

We figured it out. Barring accidents, or the unusual, she'll be here by eleven-thirty—at any rate, not later than midnight.

MRS. EPPINGWELL

(Considering.)

Not later than midnight.

CAPT. EPPINGWELL

Of course, after all, one can't tell within an hour.

Mrs. Eppingwell And she is to be brought here?

CAPT. EPPINGWELL

She'll ride the sled right up to the door. A knock, and then, enter Flossie.

MRS. EPPINGWELL

(With gratified smile.)

And then all our troubles will be over. And now for your make-up. I insist.

(Capt. Eppingwell slips off domino and stands forth a faithful copy of Sitka Charley.)

MRS. EPPINGWELL

Sitka Charley!

CAPT. EPPINGWELL

(Imitating Sitka Charley's voice.)

Um wantum dogs? I sell um dogs, much good dogs.

MRS. EPPINGWELL

(Clapping her hands.)

Excellent!

(She catches sight of Sitka Charley, who is entering through street door at rear.)

Quick!

(Helps Capt. Eppingwell on with domino.)

Now let us return to the ballroom and find Floyd Vanderlip. I'm pretty sure of him. He's in a domino, too.

(They start for exit to left. Sitka Charley, mistaking Capt. Eppingwell for Vanderlip, signals to him a desire to speak with him, but is ignored. Exit Mrs. Eppingwell and Capt. Eppingwell. Sitka Charley stands a moment, puzzled, watching them go, then follows after them. Makes, exit, and a moment later enters with Vanderlip, who is still in domino.)

VANDERLIP

(Testily.)

What do you want now?

SITKA CHARLEY

Me no want. Freda want.

VANDERLIP

What's she want?

SITKA CHARLEY

Want you.

VANDERLIP

I haven't anything to do with her. She can keep on wanting. I'm busy.

SITKA CHARLEY

Um want you now, right away, quick.

VANDERLIP

(Angrily.)

You go to the devil. And she can go, too, for all I care.

(Enter Dave Harney from left, still reading newspaper, and followed by the dancers.)

SITKA CHARLEY

I tell Freda you say go to devil?

VANDERLIP

(Flinging away angrily.)

Tell her! Tell her! Just as long as you quit bothering me.

(And then, seriously.)

And when you've told her you'd better go and see everything's in shape.

SITKA CHARLEY

(Starting for street door.)

Dogs, sleds, everything all right.

(Exit Sitka Charley.)

DAVE HARNEY

(In centre of stage, turning suddenly upon rout at his heels.)

Well? What d'ye want?

(The rout gathers about him, facing him. There are cries of: "The news! The news!" "What's happening down in God's country?" "Who won the championship?" "How'd the election turn out?" "Was Tammany downed?" "Is it true the United States is fighting Germany?" "Is war really declared?" etc.)

DAVE HARNEY

Got any sugar?

(Groans, cat-calls, and laughter.)

A Voice

The meanest man in the Klondike.

DAVE HARNEY

So you'd be, dodgast you, if you hadn't no sweetenin' for your coffee and mush.

Another Voice Speech! Speech!

Voices

Speech! Speech!

DAVE HARNEY

All right, consarn you, I'll speechify.

(Clears his throat.)

Ladies an' gentlemen—ahem—

(Stops to clear throat.)

A VOICE

Bring him some water. A glass of water, please, for the speaker.

ANOTHER VOICE

Get a box for him.

(The firewood is dumped out of the wood-box, which is placed before Dave Harney upside down. He is helped upon it.)

A VOICE

Now he's going to read us all the news. (Cheers and hand-clapping.)

DAVE HARNEY

(Folding newspaper and putting it in his pocket.)

My friend, you've got another guess comin'. I'm goin' to read you the riot act. An' here it is, short an' simple. You've got all the sugar, an' I've got all the noos. Nothin' to it but a dicker. We'll swop. That's what we'll do, we'll swop. (Cheers.)

An' I say again, for them as is dull of hearin', we'll swop. After the unmaskin', you all will assemble here in this here room an' hear the noospaper read, advertisements an' all.

(Cheers.)

An' in the meantime, I'm open to subscriptions in the form of promissory notes. Said notes shall be for the sum of one heapin', large tin cup of sugar, white or brown, to be paid to party of the first part—you all is party to the second part—to be paid to party of the first part inside twenty-four hours after the delivery of the goods, to wit, the noos. Said party of the first part hereby agreein' to send a man with a sack around to the cabins of said party of the second part an' collect face value of promissory note, to wit, one heapin', large tin cup of sugar, white or brown. Them that signs notes hears the noospaper read, them that don't, don't. Thankin' you kindly, one an' all, I remain, yours truly, an' am ready to take promissory notes here an' now.

(Cheers, laughter, and consent.)

A VOICE

But we haven't any pen or ink, Dave.

DAVE HARNEY

You've got to sit up all night to get up earlier than Dave Harney in the mornin'. Here you are.

(Draws pen, inkstand, and paper pad from pockets.)

An' you might as well sign first, young feller.

(The signing of notes begins, Dave Harney, with ink and paper, passing from one to another as the rout breaks up and starts back to ballroom for next dance.)

(Pausing in doorway to left.)

Just as easy—like shooting fish in a bucket.

(Goes out.)

(Enter Mrs. Eppingwell on arm of Vanderlip, who is still in domino. They promenade, talking, about room. They are followed by Loraine Lisznayi, masked and magnificently costumed, who keeps her eyes on them and betrays keen interest in them.)

MRS. EPPINGWELL

Wasn't it funny I guessed you, Mr. Vanderlip, in that first dance?

VANDERLIP

You have a good eye.

MRS. EPPINGWELL

And possibly I really wanted to find you, you know.

VANDERLIP

(Awkwardly, but pleased.)

Hum, yes, I suppose so. And I was looking for you, too, hard as I could.

MRS. EPPINGWELL

You'd never guess how I guessed you.

(He shakes his head.)

It is very simple. You are the same height as Captain Eppingwell.

(She laughs merrily.)

VANDERLIP

(Looking at dance-card.)

Hello, I haven't the next dance with you!

MRS. EPPINGWELL

No, that's promised to—well, to somebody else.

VANDERLIP

But the next after is mine.

MRS. EPPINGWELL

(Looking at dance-card.)

And the next after that. I'm almost afraid I'm dancing too much with you. What will people say?

VANDERLIP

(Pleased, and eagerly.)

Ah, but they don't know who we are.

MRS. EPPINGWELL

They will after the unmasking. Then they will remember us together so much.

VANDERLIP

(As though struck by a thought of something else.)

What time will they unmask?

MRS. EPPINGWELL

Two o'clock. And (Looks at card.) there is a waltz after that I should like. You do waltz so well, Mr. Vanderlip.

VANDERLIP

I won't be able to make that waltz, I—(Breaks off suddenly.)

MRS. EPPINGWELL

Why, you, of all men, are not going home early?

VANDERLIP

No—I—that is—

(Looks at card, studies it profoundly, as though it would get him out of his difficulty.)

Why, yes, of course we can have that waltz together. I thought it was already engaged, that was all.

(Enter Capt. Eppingwell, who comes up to them, still in domino.)

CAPT. EPPINGWELL

(Disguising voice.)

The next is mine, I believe, fair lady.

(Vanderlip ranges up alongside of him and measures height of shoulders. Capt. Eppingwell curiously observes the action, and speaks with gruff voice.)

Well, stranger, what's up?

VANDERLIP

We're both up.

CAPT. EPPINGWELL

Up to what?

VANDERLIP

Up to each other. We're the same height, and I've guessed you, Captain Eppingwell.

(All laugh together, and Capt. Eppingwell bears Mrs. Eppingwell away. They make exit to left.)

(Loraine accosts Vanderlip.)

LORAINE

(In disguised voice.)

A word in your ear, sir.

(Vanderlip is politely agreeable, and listens.)

All is discovered.

(He starts.)

Your actions have betrayed you.

VANDERLIP

Who are you?

LORAINE

Never mind who I am. I know.

(Takes his hand and looks at palm.) You are about to make a long journey.

(He starts.)

I see a water-hole.

(He starts.)

I hear a clock strike twelve.

(He starts.)

She is a dark woman, a foreigner.

(He starts.)

And her name is—

(In natural voice, laughing.) Loraine.

VANDERLIP

(With relief in voice.)

You fooled me all right, Loraine. You said you weren't coming to the ball.

LORAINE

I didn't intend to, but everything was packed and ready for the start, and I had nothing to do. So I came.

(A pause.)

Floyd, don't you think you've been dancing with that Mrs. Eppingwell rather frequently?

VANDERLIP

No, I don't.

LORAINE

You've danced every dance with her.

VANDERLIP

Somebody else is dancing with her now.

LORAINE

And, in consequence, you are not dancing at all.

VANDERLIP

(Making movement to take her into ballroom.)

Come, then, let us dance it together.

LORAINE

(Pouting.)

No.

VANDERLIP

(Persuasively.)

Aw, come on.

LORAINE

No.

VANDERLIP

All right, then, don't.

(He stands stolid and silent.)

LORAINE

(After a pause, softly, hesitatingly, tears in voice, etc.)

Floyd—I—

(Breaks down and weeps in feminine way.) (Vanderlip is soft as mush at once. His arm is around her, and she is drawn close to him.)

VANDERLIP

There, there, dear. You know I love you.

LORAINE

(Still weeping.)

I—I am jealous, Floyd. I know it, but I can't help it. You are a man to touch women's hearts. They can't help loving you, and—and—

VANDERLIP

(Showing that he is secretly pleased.)

Oh, pshaw. Anyway, you are the one woman, or I wouldn't be taking you down river to-night.

(Prince has gone to left and is looking into ballroom, so they are unobserved.)

LORAINE

(Recovering.)

Yes, yes, I know. Forgive me. And now I must be going.

(They move to rear to street door. He helps her on with moccasins and street wraps.) Aren't you coming, too?

VANDERLIP

(Opening door jor her.)

No, not yet. But I'll be on time.

(She glances at Prince's back, lifts mask, and raises face for kiss. He bends and kisses her.)

LORAINE

At the water-hole.

VANDERLIP

At twelve sharp.

(She kisses him again, clings to him, and goes out.)

(At sound of door shutting, Prince turns around, then returns to street door.)

PRINCE

Hello!

VANDERLIP

Hello. How d'ye like the job?

PRINCE

I wouldn't undertake it again for all the gold in Klondike.

VANDERLIP

Losing all your friends, eh?

PRINCE

Half of them. They, will butt in, and I have to turn them away. Oh, it's hospitality, you bet. I've been with them on trail, I've eaten their food and slept in their blankets, and now I turn them away from the merrymaking of myself and my friends.

(A knock is heard at door.)

There's one, now.

(Opens door.)

No, it's only Sitka Charley.

(Enter Sitka Charley, who draws Vanderlip to one side.)

SITKA CHARLEY

You come?

VANDERLIP

No, I tell you. No.

SITKA CHARLEY

No come?

VANDERLIP

(Explosively.)

NO!

SITKA CHARLEY

Then um Freda come. She say, you no come, she come. Sure.

VANDERLIP

Come here?

(He shakes his head and laughs incredulously.)

Not on your life.

SITKA CHARLEY

(Starting toward street door.)

No come?

VANDERLIP

(Explosively.)

NO!

(Exit Sitka Charley.)

(Vanderlip goes to rear, takes off domino, disclosing himself as a cowboy. Hangs domino on wall. Takes down from wall a sombrero, which he puts on head. Makes exit to left.)

(Prince, who is now alone, walks over to stove at left, adjusts damper, and warms his hands.)

(The street door is cautiously opened, without knocking, and Sitka Charley puts head inside and peers around. Withdraws head.)

(Street door is again cautiously opened, this time the masked face of a woman appearing, and then Freda, in long cloak, enters. She removes street moccasins, revealing dancing slippers on her feet, and puts moccasins under bench close to door. She removes cloak, and reveals herself in a striking evening gown. As she turns her back to hang cloak on wall, Prince happens to see her. She starts toward ballroom, but he steps in her way and stops her.)

PRINCE

I beg your pardon.

(She waits silently.)

I am the doorkeeper, you know.

(A pause.)

The instructions are that all masks must be lifted at the door.

(Still silence On part of Freda. The situation is awkward for Prince, and he begins again.)

I don't know who you are, but the rules are imperative. I must see your face.

(Steps forward and lifts his hand to raise mask.)

FREDA

(Quickly stepping back and speaking in a slightly muffled voice.)

You will be sorry if you see my face.

PRINCE

I have been made sorry by more than one face I've seen to-night and

88

turned away from the door.

FREDA

But in my case you will be sorry for quite a different reason.

PRINCE

(Curiously.)

For what reason, then, pray?

FREDA

Because, after seeing my face, you will not turn me away.

PRINCE

(With certitude.)

Then there will be no reason for me to turn you away.

FREDA

On the contrary, all the reason in the world. But you won't.

(Prince laughs incredulously. Mrs. Mc-Fee appears in doorway to left, looks suspiciously at them, and disappears.)

So it will be better, Stanley, if you let me in without seeing my face.

PRINCE

(Starting at her use of his given name.) You know me!—er—well!

FREDA

And you know me well. Now let me pass. Some day I will tell you about it, my reason for coming here, and you will be glad.

(She starts as though to go to the ballroom.)

PRINCE

(Springing in her way and seizing her arm.)

No you don't, my lady! Enough fooling. Let me see your face.

FREDA

There have been times when you treated me less roughly. For the sake of those times, let me pass.

PRINCE

(Still retaining hold on her arm, and after hesitating for a moment.)

No, it's a bluff you're running on me. I don't know who you are, but I'm going to find out.

(He lifts free hand toward her mask.)

FREDA

You will be sorry.

(He hesitates.)

Be in ignorance of me, and let me pass. It will be better so.

PRINCE

If you have no right, I'll not let you pass anyway. Now let me see you.

(Still holding her by one arm, he tries to lift mask.)

(Mrs. McFee appears in doorway to left and watches suspiciously.)

(Sitka Charley knocks and then enters through street door, Prince giving a quick glance in his direction and ascertaining that it is all right for him to enter.)

FREDA

(In natural voice.)

Stanley!

PRINCE

(Releasing her and speaking with awe.) No! Not you!

(Freda lifts her mask, her back to Mrs. McFee, and for several seconds, her face serious with resolve, her eyes flashing, she gazes upon him. She lowers mask, and makes as though to start toward door to left. He hesitates, stands aside, then hesitates again.)

It is all my social standing in Dawson is worth, to—to let you pass.

FREDA

(Mockingly.)

I told you-you would be sorry.

(Seriously.)

There is Sitka Charley. I want to speak to him. And there's that psalm-singer in the doorway. Don't let her suspect me.

PRINCE

I shall resign my post.

FREDA

Resign? You will be of more help to me if you retain it.

PRINCE

I have been unfaithful to it. Pass, Freda, pass. Who am I to say you nay?

(He leaves her and returns to street door. Freda goes over to Sitka Charley. Mrs. McFee disappears jrom doorway, but reappears one or two times to stare suspiciously.)

FREDA

How is Vanderlip dressed? What does he look like?

SITKA CHARLEY

Um all the same long black dress, like um woman.

FREDA

Dressed as a woman!

SITKA CHARLEY

(Shaking his head.)

No dress woman. Um like—um—um—like um priest man.

(Makes motion of hand around head to describe hood of domino, and motion down to his feet to describe length of domino.)

Um long black, like priest man.

(A domino, with lady on arm, appears in doorway, as though about to enter, then changing mind, disappears.)

Look see! Just like that. That um Vanderlip.

FREDA

All right, Charley. I understand. And now for you. Flossie can't get here too quickly. You must take dogs, fresh dogs, up the trail, and when you meet her, put her on your sled, and race in with her as fast as you can. Tell her Vanderlip sent you and is waiting for her.

SITKA CHARLEY

(Dubiously.)

Um dogs, fresh dogs, have not got.

FREDA

Take my dogs. You know them.

SITKA CHARLEY

(Enthusiastically.)

Um best dogs in Klondike. Sure.

FREDA

And bring Flossie straight to my cabin. Don't stop anywhere else for anything. Right up to the door and in with her. Understand?

SITKA CHARLEY

Um Vanderlip there?

FREDA

Yes, Vanderlip will be there waiting for her.

(Starts him toward street door.)

Now hurry.

(Exit Sitka Charley.)

(To Prince, who is standing forlornly at his post.)

I'm sorry, Stanley, but I had to do this thing. Now I want to find Floyd Vanderlip.

PRINCE

You'll find him in the ballroom. Black domino—you know his height.

FREDA

(Resting one hand on his arm and laughing cheerily.)

There, there, don't look so glum. All is not lost. Nobody will know me, and I'll be gone in five minutes.

(Mrs. McFee appears in doorway to left. Looks at them standing together.)

(Freda crosses to left and goes out, Mrs. McFee standing aside and looking at her closely.)

(Mrs. McFee crosses to Prince.)

MRS. McFEE

Who might that woman be, Mr. Prince?

PRINCE

(Coldly.)

The doorkeeper's lips are sealed. Those were my instructions. The doorkeeper can disclose identities to nobody.

MRS. McFEE

But to me—

PRINCE

(Interrupting icily.)

To nobody. You are made no exception, Mrs. McFee. And furthermore, I'm going to resign.

MRS. McFEE

Resign!

PRINCE

And right now. And whoever takes my place—you'd better put a mask on him, or he'll lose all his friends as I have.

MRS. MCFEE

(Insinuatingly.)

Your friends, the kind of men and women you turned from this door?

PRINCE

(Angrily.)

Yes, my friends, men and women, children of sin, lost, hopeless wretches,—my friends.

MRS. McFEE

(Sniffing and tossing her head, and very frigidly.)

I believe it is just as well, Mr. Prince. I had my doots of you all along. There is no telling what base creatures you have admitted. I shall get an honorable man to guard the door. I shall inform the committee—

PRINCE

(Interrupting.)

Get him! Get him! Go get him! You can't be any too quick for me!

MRS. MCFEE

(Beginning angrily.)

You are a shame and a disgrace, and when I bring your conduct before the committee—

PRINCE

(Interrupting.)

If you don't go right away and get some one to take my place, I'll throw open the door and call in the scum of the town.

(Makes a motion to open door.)

MRS. McFEE

(Aghast, throwing up arms.)

No! No! Dinna be rash!

(She hastens away into ballroom.)

(Several couples have entered from ballroom and are promenading, among them Capt. Eppingwell, by himself, in domino.) (Enter Sitka Charley through street door, looking for some one. He mistakes Capt. Eppingwell for Vanderlip.)

SITKA CHARLEY

Hello, Vanderlip. You no come Freda's cabin you catch um hell, sure.

CAPT. EPPINGWELL

(Starting, and in disguised voice.)

Hello. What's Freda want with me.

SITKA CHARLEY

(Recognizing that it is not Vanderlip's voice, and surprised.)

You no Vanderlip?

CAPT. EPPINGWELL

(Imitating Sitka Charley's voice.)

No. Me Sitka Charley.

SITKA CHARLEY

What for, crazymans? Me Sitka Charley.

CAPT. EPPINGWELL

Me Sitka Charley.

SITKA CHARLEY

No, me.

CAPT. EPPINGWELL

No, me.

(He suddenly takes off domino, disclosing himself in make-up of Sitka Charley. Sitka Charley gazes at him dumbfounded. Rubs his eyes.)

You buy um dogs, good dogs, I sell.

SITKA CHARLEY

You me. Who me?

(Rubs his eyes.)

What for? Everybody crazy. Me crazy too.

CAPT. EPPINGWELL

(Struck by an idea, he puts on domino again, and drags Sitka Charley by arm to back of room.)

Come on, we'll have some fun.

(Feels in pocket of overcoat hanging on wall and brings out a mask, which he puts on Sitka Charley.)

Now for fun!

(Capt. Eppingwell takes Sitka Charley to left, thrusts him into ballroom, and remains in doorway, watching.)

(Enter Freda. Capt. Eppingwell stands aside for her to pass. But she stops and measures his height and build with her eye.)

FREDA

(Softly.)

At last I've found you, Floyd.

CAPT. EPPINGWELL

I like that, guessing me the first time. And who are you?

FREDA

(Surprised.)

Oh! It was a mistake.

(Starts to leave him, but he follows her, detaining her.)

CAPT. EPPINGWELL

Not so fast, fair lady. I've an idea you'll dance—

(Looks at his dance-card.)

—the next quadrille, let us say.

FREDA

I think it's engaged. I've lost my programme.

CAPT. EPPINGWELL

(Putting hand inside domino and bringing forth a programme.)

I have a spare one. Allow me.

(He writes on card.)

(Enter Sitka Charley from left, running away from Clown, who is striking him on back with bladder.)

FREDA

Thank you. The next quadrille then. (Looking at Sitka Charley.)

There is somebody I wish to speak to. Good-by.

CAPT. EPPINGWELL

(Standing aside.)

Good-by.

(Mrs. McFee enters from left with man, whom she takes to street door and who relieves Prince, who makes exit to left.)

(Freda joins in pursuit of Sitka Charley and drives Clown away.)

(Mrs. McFee watches Freda and Sitka Charley.)

FREDA

(Severely.)

I thought you had started up the trail with the dogs long ago. Anything the matter?

SITKA CHARLEY

Me come back speak to you. Me think, um Lisznayi woman wait at water-hole, no Vanderlip come, maybe she make much trouble. Much better Lisznayi woman go long way off. Maybe I think very good tell Lisznayi woman lie. Maybe say Vanderlip meet her twenty mile down trail. One Indian man take her on sled twenty mile down trail, then she sure make no trouble.

FREDA

(Laughing.)

A good idea. You hurry and fix it up, quick, and then start after Flossie.

(Sitka Charley starts to go.)

One moment, Charley. Ten miles down river is Salmon Stake. One missionary man lives at Salmon Stake. Tell Indian man to take Lisznayi woman to missionary house and knock on door. Missionary man gets out of bed and lets them in. Indian man tells missionary man that Lisznayi woman come to see him, come to be good woman.

(She laughs merrily.)

Understand?

SITKA CHARLEY

(Laughing silently.)

Very good. Dam good. All right.

FREDA

(Turning to leave him.)

And hurry as fast as you can.

(Freda, looking over one after another of couples and groups, and watched suspiciously by Mrs. McFee, continues search for Vanderlip and goes to left.)

(Sitka Charley starts toward street door, but is interrupted by Mrs. McFee.)

MRS. MCFEE

Who is that woman?

SITKA CHARLEY

Um crazy womans maybe.

MRS. McFEE

But who is she?

SITKA CHARLEY

(Stirring the air with his hand to describe general mix-up.)

Everybody somebody; somebody nobody; nobody anybody. What for? Sitka Charley no Sitka Charley. Sitka Charley somebody else. Somebody else Sitka Charley.

MRS. McFEE

(With a sour smile of appreciation.)

You do it very well. Allow me to congratulate you.

SITKA CHARLEY

What for long words? Sitka Charley don't know long words.

MRS. McFEE

Oh, I know you, Captain Eppingwell.

SITKA CHARLEY

Me no Captain Eppingwell. Me Sitka Charley.

MRS. MCFEE

You do it excellently. Even I would be almost deceived, I assure you, Captain Eppingwell.

SITKA CHARLEY

Me Captain Eppingwell?

MRS. McFEE

Of course you are. I knew you at once.

SITKA CHARLEY

Mrs. Eppingwell my squaw?

MRS. MCFEE

Yes, and Mrs. Eppingwell is your wife. Now tell me who that woman was.

SITKA CHARLEY

(After holding head in both hands.)

Me no drink whiskey all day. Yet me all the same drunk. Me no me. Me Captain Eppingwell. Me have one fine squaw. Wow! (Soberly, holding one hand to head and shaking head.)

Sitka Charley much sick. Sitka Charley go home. (Starts for street door, but Mrs. McFee detains him.)

MRS. McFEE

No, no, Captain, you are coming with me to see how the supper is being laid, and you are going to tell me who that woman is.

(Sitka Charley does not want to go, but, vainly protesting, is lugged off by Mrs. McFee through door to left.)

(Capt. Eppingwell, who has lingered about, watches them got and when gone he takes off domino, hangs same on wall, and discloses himself in make-up of Sitka Charley. He proceeds to put wood in stove to right.)

(Freda enters from left and sees Capt. Eppingwell bending over woodbox. She crosses over to him in an angry, determined way.)

FREDA

(Very severely.)

Still here! When I asked you to hurry!

(Capt. Eppingwell straightens up abruptly.)

Scorn of Women

Shame on you, Charley. Now go, as fast as you can.

CAPT. EPPINGWELL

(Imitating Sitka Charley.)

What for go? You buy dogs? I sell dogs, good dogs.

FREDA

(With petulant dismay.)

Oh! You again!

CAPT. EPPINGWELL

Me Sitka Charley.

FREDA

You are the man in the domino. I might have known you were not Sitka Charley. You are taller.

CAPT. EPPINGWELL

(Natural voice.)

And in the domino you mistook me because of my height.

(Freda starts.)

Oh, I know. The man you seek is about my height, eh?

FREDA

Who are you?

CAPT. EPPINGWELL

Who are you?

FREDA

You don't know me. I am a new arrival in Dawson. I came in over the ice.

102

CAPT. EPPINGWELL

(With sudden conviction.)

Now I have you! I met you to-day.

FREDA

(Shaking head.)

No, you didn't.

CAPT. EPPINGWELL

Yes, I did. You are the Lisznayi—I beg pardon—Miss—er—Miss Lisznayi.

FREDA

(Simulating surrender.)

It's a shame to be found out so quickly. Mister—? Mister—?

CAPT. EPPINGWELL

Mr. Sitka Charley.

FREDA

Well, then, Mr. Sitka Charley, I am displeased with you. You are too cunning. I am really vexed, and for punishment I am going to leave you.

(She curtsies deeply, and walks away toward left.)

CAPT. EPPINGWELL

(To himself, as he watches her.)

That voice. That walk! That carriage!

(Scratches head, then suddenly.)

Fooled! Fooled! That's not the Lisznayi!

(He springs after her.)

(A voice, off stage, is heard calling, "Take partners for a quadrille!")

I beg pardon, but this dance is ours.

FREDA

(Drawing watch and looking at it.)

Yes, it is, but really, I must beg off. I—I don't like quadrilles.

(Looks at dance-card.)

There's a waltz two dances down. I'll give you that.

(A man, in costume, appears in doorway to left, and shouts: "One more couple needed! Here, you! One more couple!")

CAPT. EPPINGWELL

(Offering his arm.)

There! We're needed.

(Man in doorway, who has turned around and surveyed ballroom, turns back and calls: "Too late! Sets are full!" Opening bars of dance are heard.)

CAPT. EPPINGWELL

(Seizing Freda in his arms and starting to waltz.)

We'll make a waltz of it here.

(They waltz a jew steps, Freda abandoning herself to it, when she suddenly stops and withdraws herselj from his arms.)

FREDA

Please let me go. You may have that waltz later.

(She looks at watch and betrays her need for haste.)

CAPT. EPPINGWELL

(Very deliberately.)

There is something familiar about you. I have seen you before. I have danced with you before. And—well, I have never danced with the Lisznayi.

FREDA

No, you don't know me.

CAPT. EPPINGWELL

Let me tell you the occasion.

FREDA

(Very restless and desiring to go.)

There has been no occasion.

CAPT. EPPINGWELL

(Firmly.)

Nevertheless, let me tell you. It may interest you.

(Makes appropriate gestures.)

Here was the stove, here the piano. Three-fingered Jack played the fiddle. It was Old Dan Tucker that we danced. Remember?

(She shakes her head.)

There was the doorway to the front, always open. Through it came the clatter of chips, the rattle of roulette balls, the calls of the gamekeepers. And there was the rear door. It opened upon the street. When it opened the frost came through, in a cloud of vapor, rolling along the floor and hiding the feet and legs of the dancers to the knees. And we danced, you and I, we danced Old Dan Tucker.

FREDA

(Innocently.)

How interesting! Tell me, that—that what you described, it is a—a dance-hall? Am I right?

CAPT. EPPINGWELL

(With firm conviction.)

I remember when you came in through the door. The frost rolled in with you, and you wore the most magnificent furs in all the Klondike. And you danced in moccasins, in little red moccasins. Remember?

FREDA

(Still innocently.)

Ah, those furs! Is there a woman in the land who has not heard of them and envied their possessor, this woman you take me for—and I know who you mean—this—this dance-hall artist, this—this Freda Moloof. And how often have you danced with her?—with me, I mean.

CAPT. EPPINGWELL

(Shaken for the moment.)

Once. That one night. But I have seen her several times. Who has not?

FREDA

Her? Me, you mean.

CAPT. EPPINGWELL

(With renewed and emphatic conviction.)

Yes, and one other thing. That accent!

(Gripping her by the arm.)

Freda, it is you!

FREDA

At last I am discovered. Confess, sir, it took you some time.

CAPT. EPPINGWELL

I do confess you puzzled me not a little. But what are you doing here?

It's daring, to say the least.

FREDA

(Nonchalantly.)

Oh, I was weary for a change. I was yawning my head off. So I thought I'd come up and see if you and your select friends danced Old Dan Tucker as well as we danced it that—that night.

CAPT. EPPINGWELL

But if you are discovered?

FREDA

Only you could discover me.

CAPT. EPPINGWELL

(With due hesitancy.)

There is trouble brewing, Freda. Frankly, I believe it would be better for you to go.

(Freda laughs long, a mocking, silvery laughter which perplexes and bewilders him.)

Come, come. What's the matter?

(Freda continues to laugh.)

What's struck you so funny?

FREDA

(Quieting down, but holding hand to side.) It is better than I dreamed.

CAPT. EPPINGWELL

What is better?

FREDA

My make-up.

Capt. Eppingwell (In doubt.)

Make-up?

FREDA

The make-up under my make-up, if you please.

CAPT. EPPINGWELL

(With a faint glimmer of conviction this time.)

But the accent! You can't get away from it.

FREDA

Far be it from me to get away from it. On the contrary, I sought after it, and I flatter myself that I got it pretty close to the original. I'd like to meet this Freda. I'll wager my accent is nearer hers than her own is.

CAPT. EPPINGWELL

(Completely beaten, slowly.)

Then who the deuce are you? Where could you have learned that accent?

FREDA

(As one will tell a story.)

Why, I was caught in a storm over on Indian River. We were compelled to seek shelter in a little cabin, and whom should we find there, likewise driven in by the storm, but this Freda Moloof. There was no standing on ceremony nor conventionality. It was life or death, and in I went. We were storm-bound two days. And she was very kind to me.

(A pause, then, voice tender and sympathetic.)

I felt so sorry for her.

(A pause.)

CAPT. EPPINGWELL

(Impatiently.)

Well?

FREDA

Well, I studied her, that is all.

CAPT. EPPINGWELL

(Triumphantly.)

Now I have you! You are the woman reporter of the Kansas City Star!

FREDA

(Mockingly.)

Think so? Think so?

(She laughs.)

Now I am really going to leave you. I must. But don't forget that waltz.

(She walks away and makes exit to left.)

CAPT. EPPINGWELL

(In utter bewilderment, watching her till she disappears.)

Well, I'll be damned.

(He puts on domino and follows after her, still intent on discovering her identity, and makes exit to left.)

(The quadrille is over, and as he passes out, couples begin to enter from left.)

(Mrs. McFee and Sitka Charley enter from left. She still holds him captive, hanging on his arm.)

MRS. McFEE

(Ingratiatingly, making as near a simper as her sour mouth and age will permit.) You might have asked me to dance, Captain.

SITKA CHARLEY

(Rolling his head.)

Me no dance. Me much sick. Me crazy. Me drunk. Me go home.

(Strives to get to street door, but she clings to his arm and holds him back.)

MRS. McFEE

Dinna you think by now, Captain, that you've convinced me what a fine actor you are?

SITKA CHARLEY

(Striving for street door, but being held back, in final break-down of patience.)

What for, dam fool woman you?

MRS. McFEE

(Dropping his arm and recoiling.)

Oh!

SITKA CHARLEY

(In a rage, dancing about.)

Crazy! Fool! Dam! What for?

MRS. McFEE

Oh! Oh! And I thought you were a gentleman! You have insulted me!

SITKA CHARLEY

(Raging.)

Sure! Me insult. Much insult. Dam! Dam! Dam!

110

MRS. McFEE

Oh! This cannot be Captain Eppingwell. 'Tis some base creature from the town. I am contameenated!

(Sticks fingers in ears and screams shrilly.) (Many come running from ballroom at sound of screams. Sitka Charley still rages, shouting, "Dam! Dam! Dam!")

(Capt. Eppingwell comes in with some lady on arm and joins an onlooking group near stove to right. He still wears domino.)

MRS. McFEE

(To onlookers.)

This vile creature has insulted me. Where is the doorkeeper?

(Turns and beckons Doorkeeper.)

Come you, Mr. McFarline, and eject this beast.

(Doorkeeper starts forward. Clown startles Sitka Charley by unexpectedly hitting him a resounding blow with bladder between the shoulders. Sitka Charley runs in and out amongst people, pursued by Doorkeeper and Clown. The Doorkeeper is slow and ponderous, and falls down. At the moment he falls, Sitka Charley dashes into group where stands Capt. Eppingwell, whom he strips, with one rush, of domino. Sitka Charley swiftly puts domino on himself and dashes, on, still pursued by Clown, who is striking him with bladder. Both make exit to left.)

(Doorkeeper, getting up, mistakes Capt. Eppingwell for Sitka Charley, and proceeds to eject him. Capt. Eppingwell resists. Mrs. McFee urges on the Doorkeeper. In struggle, Capt. Eppingwell's mask comes off. Doorkeeper, in amazement, lets go of him. Capt. Eppingwell is angry, Mrs. McFee dumfounded, everybody excited.—Tableau.)

(Sitka Charley dashes in from left, pursued by Clown. Sitka Charley races madly across stage, like a dog with a tin can to its tail, and jerks open street door. Doorkeeper tries to stop him, clutches domino, but Sitka Charley plunges through and slams door after him, leaving domino in hands of Doorkeeper, who is nonplussed for a moment, then walks over and presents it to Capt. Eppingwell.)

(Excitement quiets down. Groups break up and begin to pass off stage to left.)

(Capt. Eppingwell, having lingered in order to recover his breath, goes to left rear and hangs up domino on wall.)

(Vanderlip, in costume of cowboy, and Mrs. Eppingwell are standing talking by stove to right front.)

(Freda enters alone from left and looks about. Recognizes Capt. Eppingwell and goes up to him.)

Capt. Eppingwell (Gallantly.)

Ah, mysterious fair one!

FREDA

(Lightly.)

Surely you have guessed me by now.

CAPT. EPPINGWELL

(Shaking head sadly.)

I was never so befooled in my life. I could swear I know you, but to save me I can't put my finger on you.

FREDA

You may if you wish.

CAPT. EPPINGWELL

(Surprised.)

What?

FREDA

(Seriously.)

I say you may know me if you wish.

CAPT. EPPINGWELL

(Eagerly.)

How?—When?

FREDA

Now.

(He eagerly makes to lift mask and learn her identity. She steps hand quickly, with one hand holding him off.)

No, no; there are certain stipulations.

CAPT. EPPINGWELL

(Displaying in advance a willingness to consent.)

Yes, yes.

FREDA

(Deliberately.)

First, you must ask no questions.

(He nods head.)

Second, you must tell nobody.

(He nods.)

And third, you must point out to me Floyd Vanderlip.

CAPT. EPPINGWELL

(Nodding head.)

I agree. Now who are you?

FREDA

(Laughing.)

But you haven't pointed out Floyd Vanderlip.

CAPT. EPPINGWELL

(Briskly, indicating with his head.)

There he is.

FREDA

(Looking.)

And with whom is he talking?

CAPT. EPPINGWELL

(Starting as though to answer, then changing his mind.)

That was not in the bond. Now who are you?

FREDA

(Mockingly.)

Guess.

CAPT. EPPINGWELL

I call that cruel. I've exhausted my guesses. (Freda lifts mask and gazes at him for several seconds, her face serious, her eyes flashing.)

CAPT. EPPINGWELL

(Giving a long whistle of comprehension.) Freda!

FREDA

Even so, Freda. And I thank you. And I shall have yet more to thank you for. That waltz—you must let me off.

Capt. Eppingwell There is no reason. Let me have it.

FREDA

Impossible. I shall be gone.

(Looks at watch.)

Why, it is half-past eleven! I am going now, in a minute.

Capt. Eppingwell With Vanderlip?

FREDA

With Vanderlip.

Capt. Eppingwell (Earnestly.)

Freda, do you know all the circumstances of this—er—affair? Do you know what you are doing?

FREDA

(Lightly.)....

You are asking questions, sir. It is not in the bond.

Capt. Eppingwell (Giving in.)

Right. I beg your pardon.

(A knock is heard at street door. Doorkeeper opens. Enter messenger, an Indian, in parka and trail costume. He appears tired. He looks about hesitatingly, dazzled by the lights.)

CAPT. EPPINGWELL

(Recognizing messenger, to Freda.) Pardon me, please, a moment. I must speak to that man.

(Walks over to Indian.).

How soon she come?

INDIAN

Come soon. Much dogs. Come fast. One hour maybe. Maybe half-hour.

CAPT. EPPINGWELL

All right. Come along.

(Walks to Mrs. Eppingwell and Vanderlip at stove at right front, Indian at his heels.)

Here's that man I told you of, Maud. You had better speak with him—I beg your pardon, Vanderlip.

VANDERLIP

(Jovially.)

That's all right. Business is business.

MRS. EPPINGWELL

(Sweetly.)

Oh, Mr. Vanderlip, I left my programme on the piano, and I really don't know with whom I have the next dance. Please.

(She steps aside with Indian to talk.)

(Vanderlip starts toward exit to left.) (Capt. Eppingwell starts to rejoin Freda.) (Freda starts to cut off Vanderlip, crossing Capt. Eppingwell.)

CAPT. EPPINGWELL

(Softly.)

Oh, Freda! That waltz.

FREDA

One moment, please.

(Passes on to Vanderlip.)

(Capt. Eppingwell stands gazing.)

(A dance has finished, and couples begin to stray in.)

(Clown and a lady accost Capt. Eppingwell, and the three move along together.)

(Mrs. McFee enters. As she passes by, she looks hard and suspiciously at Freda.)

FREDA

Come with me, Floyd. I want you now.

VANDERLIP

(With mock politeness.)

And who are you, may I ask?

FREDA

Freda.

VANDERLIP

(Beginning explosively.)

What the—

(Then breaking down.)

My God, Freda, what have you come here for?

FREDA

For you.

VANDERLIP

(Hesitatingly.)

I don't understand. You are nothing to me.

FREDA

And never have been anything, remember that, Floyd.

(Conveying the impression that she may be something to him in the immediate future.) But I want you now.

VANDERLIP

And never will be anything, I assure you. (Getting back his courage.)
Faugh! What have you come here for, anyway?

FREDA

For you. And, moreover, you are going to come with me. You are going to let me take your arm, and you see that door there—you are going to take me out through it.

VANDERLIP

(Bellicosely.)

I see myself doing it.

FREDA

Yes, and I see you going on to my cabin.

VANDERLIP

(Interested, curiously.)

To your cabin?

FREDA

Yes, to my cabin. I want to talk with you.

VANDERLIP

This is a good place right here. Talk away.

FREDA

No, you must come with me.

VANDERLIP

(Obstinately.)

Not on your life, Freda. Right here I stay.

FREDA

118

You have seen a little of me, Floyd; but you have heard more of me.

VANDERLIP

(Interrupting.)

Oh, yes, I have heard that you play with men as a child plays with bubbles. It is a saying in the country. Well,

(Planting himself firmly.)

I am no bubble.

FREDA

(Quietly.)

What time is it, Floyd?

VANDERLIP

(Looking at watch, startled.)

Twenty-five to twelve! Gee! I've got to get out of this!

(Makes a hasty movement, as though to start toward street door. Freda takes his arm.)

What's this?

FREDA

Nothing. Come along. I am in a hurry.

VANDERLIP

Now look here, Freda, I'm not going with you because you're making me. I've got to go anyway. I've got to be elsewhere, and pretty quick.

FREDA

Oh, far from it. I never make anybody do anything. They just—do it.

VANDERLIP

All right, I'll let you come with me, but only outside. I'm not going to your cabin.

FREDA

That is for you to determine. Let us start.

(Mrs. Eppingwell talks with Indian. Mrs. Eppingwell now and again glances anxiously at Freda and Vanderlip; Mrs. McFee is more suspicious than ever, her hands involuntarily clutching and unclutching as though with desire to spring upon Freda and held back only by doubt.)

VANDERLIP

(Absently.)

'I'll have to rush. Got to change my clothes—

FREDA

(Interrupting.)

Not for my cabin. Those clothes are good enough.

VANDERLIP

(Angrily.)

But I tell you I am not going to your cabin.

FREDA

Oh, well, never mind. The first thing is to get out of here. After that we'll see.

VANDERLIP

(Defiantly.)

You bet we'll see.

(They start toward street door, Freda on his arm.)

MRS. EPPINGWELL

(Hurriedly, to Capt. Eppingwell.)

Who is that woman?

CAPT. EPPINGWELL

(Awkwardly.)

How should I know?

MRS. EPPINGWELL

(Reproachfully, and hurriedly.)

Archie! I saw her lift her mask to you a moment ago.

CAPT. EPPINGWELL

I can't tell—I—she—

(Mrs. Eppingwell does not listen further, but hastens to cut off Freda and Vanderlip.)

FREDA

(Seeing Mrs. Eppingwell approaching.) If anybody stops me, Floyd, I shall quarrel, I know.

VANDERLIP

(Frightened.)

For goodness' sake, don't make a scene.

FREDA

Then get me out of here quick. Don't stop. (But Vanderlip stops when cut off by Mrs. Eppingwell.)

MRS. EPPINGWELL

I beg pardon. You are not going, Mr. Vanderlip?

VANDERLIP

(Awkwardly.)

I—yes, I'm going.

Mrs. Eppingwell But those dances?

VANDERLIP

(Hiding embarrassment behind brusqueness.)

I've suddenly recollected something. I'm in a hurry. Please excuse me, Mrs. Eppingwell.

(Freda starts at mention of name.)

MRS. EPPINGWELL

(Reproachfully.)

And you promised to take me in to supper.

VANDERLIP

Of course, of course. And I will. I'll come back.

MRS. EPPINGWELL

I'd rather you didn't go—Floyd. The next dance

(Looking at his card.) is ours. It will begin in a minute.

(Vanderlip does not know what to say. Freda urges him to continue toward door by tugging privily on his arm. Also she glances apprehensively at Mrs. McFee, who, with a set expression on face, has drawn nearer.)

VANDERLIP

(Hesitatingly.)

Really, Mrs. Eppingwell, I—

FREDA

(Interrupting, urging him by arm to start toward door.)

We'll be late. We must go.

(Vanderlip half starts to go with her toward door.)

MRS. EPPINGWELL

(To Freda.)

I beg pardon, but you scarcely understand.

FREDA

(Sharply, overwrought nervously.)

It would be better, Mrs. Eppingwell, did your husband understand as well as I.

(Mrs. Eppingwell is visibly hurt, and for the moment shocked into silence.)

VANDERLIP

Now, look here, I'm not going to have any quarrelling between you women.

MRS. EPPINGWELL

(With sudden suspicion, ignoring Vanderlip.)

Who are you?

FREDA

(Coldly.)

One whose existence would scarcely interest you, Mrs. Eppingwell.

VANDERLIP

(Whose efforts to make peace are ignored.) Oh, I say—

(Mrs. McFee has drawn nearer. Everybody on stage is interested.)

Mrs. Eppingwell I have the right to know.

FREDA

(Scathingly.)

As custodian of the community's morals?

MRS. EPPINGWELL

And why not?

FREDA

(Mockingly.)

Ah, and why not?

MRS. EPPINGWELL

(With energy, but coolly and collectedly.)

You have the advantage. You know who I am. Who are you? I demand to know.

(Freda laughs lightly and mockingly.)

MRS. McFEE

(Entering group with a very determined air and pausing an instant.)

We'll settle that, Mrs. Eppingwell.

(Mrs. McFee suddenly springs upon Freda, tearing mask jrom face. Freda is startled and frightened. Vanderlip, the situation beyond him, stares helplessly back and forth between Freda and Mrs. Eppingwell. Everybody on the stage stares at Freda, forming a wide and irregular circle of onlookers, who are too polite to crowd closer, but who, nevertheless, cannot resist staring, one and all, from a distance.)

MRS. MCFEE

(Sarcastically, shrilly.)

Mrs. Eppingwell, it is with great pleasure I make you acquainted with

Freda Moloof—Miss Freda Moloof, as I understand.

(Mrs. Eppingwell makes a gesture to silence Mrs. McFee, who pauses for a moment.)

Mayhap you dinna know the lady. Let me tell you—

VANDERLIP

(Interrupting.)

Now, here, I say, what's the good—

MRS. McFEE

(Interrupting, and withering him with a look.)

Child of Perdition!

(She continues.)

As I was saying, this woman's antecedents—a dancing girl, a destroyer of men's souls, a bold, brazen hussy, a servant of Satan, a—

Mrs. Eppingwell (Interrupting.)

That will do, Mrs. McFee. Will you please leave me to talk with her?

(Mrs. McFee, still holding mask, snorts and withdraws a step from group.)

FREDA

(Quickly, excitedly, eyes flashing.)

I do not want you to talk with me. What more can you say than that woman (Indicating Mrs. McFee, who snorts.) has said? I want to go. Come on, Floyd.

MRS. EPPINGWELL

(Gently.)

I do not wish to be harsh.

FREDA

(On verge oj tears, yet dry-eyed and resolute.)

Be anything but kind. That I will not bear.

Mrs. Eppingwell (Beginning gently.)

I—

FREDA

(Interrupting, excitedly.)

It is you that have the advantage now, hiding behind that mask. Your face is clothed. I am as naked before you, (Glancing around masked circle and shrinking as a naked woman might shrink.) before all of you.

MRS. EPPINGWELL

But you should not have come here.

FREDA

I had reason to come.

MRS. EPPINGWELL

An evil reason, I fear. However—

(She calmly removes her own mask.)

(For a long moment they regard each other with fixed gaze, Freda aggressive, meteoric, at bay; Mrs. Eppingwell calm-eyed, serene, dispassionate. Freda begins to soften.)

FREDA

(Softly.)

You are kind.

MRS. EPPINGWELL

No; it is merely fair play.

MRS. McFEE

(Bursting out wrathfully.)

Why dinna you tell the hussy to go?

MRS. EPPINGWELL

(Masterfully.)

Be quiet.

FREDA

(Breaking down, seeming to droop for an instant, with one short dry sob or catch in the throat.)

Yes, I will go, Mrs. Eppingwell.

(Turning to Vanderlip.)

Will you come, Floyd?

(Vanderlip looks to Mrs. Eppingwell for consent.)

MRS. EPPINGWELL

Mr. Vanderlip will stay.

(Freda, broken down, beaten, but with no tears, no wringing of hands, nor customary signs of feminine weakness, with head up, mechanically resolute and defiant, ordinary carriage and speed of walk, goes toward street door. Silence. Everybody watches her. Doorkeeper does not assist her when she gropes blindly under bench for street moccasins.)

(What is emphasized is her isolation. She is not one of them, and they regard her as they would regard a strange animal which had strayed in out of the night.)

(She sits down on bench to put on street moccasins. Just as she lifts her foot to put on first moccasin, she pauses, thinks, then puts foot down again. She puts down moccasins, stands up, pauses irresolutely a moment, then walks forward to Mrs. Eppingwell and Vanderlip.)

FREDA

(Quietly.)

Mrs. Eppingwell, pardon me, but I had forgotten for the moment what I came for.

MRS. EPPINGWELL

And that is—?

FREDA

Floyd Vanderlip.

VANDERLIP

(Angrily.)

Now look here, Freda, I tell you I won't stand for this.

(Freda ignores him.)

Mrs. Eppingwell I trust, Miss Moloof—

FREDA

(Interrupting.)

Call me Freda.

(Bitterly.)

Everybody calls me Freda.

MRS. EPPINGWELL

Well, Freda, then. Have you thought what you are doing? It is an awkward thing to play with souls. What right have you?

FREDA

(Laughing harshly.)

Right? I have no rights. Only privileges.

MRS. EPPINGWELL

(With touch of anger.)

Licenses, I should say.

(Mrs. McFee snorts and approaches.)

FREDA

Thank you, licenses. I have licenses which you have not, for, you see, you are the wife of a captain.

MRS. EPPINGWELL

What do you want with this man?

FREDA

I might ask what you want with him? You have your husband.

MRS. EPPINGWELL

And you?

FREDA

(Wearily.)

Men, just men.

MRS. EPPINGWELL

(Anger growing.)

You are all that has been said of you, a destroyer of men.

FREDA

(Nodding her head in assent.)

Come on, Floyd. I want you. And be warned by Mrs. Eppingwell, I want to destroy you. (Imperiously.)

Come.

(Vanderlip has by now been reduced to the helplessness of a puppet. He makes to start.)

MRS. EPPINGWELL

(Imperiously.)

Floyd Vanderlip, you remain where you are. (He stops.)

FREDA

(Almost whispering.)

Come.

(He makes to start.)

MRS. EPPINGWELL

(Warningly, imperiously.) Floyd!

(He stops.)

MRS. McFEE

(To Vanderlip, witheringly, imitating his hesitancy by bobbing her body.)

You weak and sinful creature, bobbing here, and bobbing there, like a chicken with its head cut off!

VANDERLIP

(Stirred to sudden flame of anger.)

Once for all, Freda, I'm not going with you.

FREDA

(Quietly.)

What time is it, Floyd?

VANDERLIP

(Looking at watch, startled.)

Quarter to twelve! I must go, Mrs. Eppingwell. Good-by.

(He starts toward door at heels of Freda, who leads him by a couple of steps.)

MRS. EPPINGWELL

Shame on you,

(Freda glances back and smiles a hard smile.)

FREDA MOLOOF.

(Calling softly.)

Floyd!

(Vanderlip hesitates. Freda turns her face, blazingly imperious, upon him, and he slinks on after her. Dead silence.)

(When they reach door.)

Help me on with my moccasins, Floyd.

(He hesitates, with a last faint spark of rebellion. She looks at him, blazingly imperious.)

There they are.

(He is beaten. Stoops for moccasins. She sits down on bench. He puts moccasins on her feet. They stand up. He helps her on with her cloak. While he is putting on his own moccasins and a big bearskin overcoat, she pulls hood of cloak over her head and covering her ears. Then she puts on her mittens. Then she waits for him. He puts on cap and mittens and opens street door.)

(Recollecting, and turning toward Mrs. McFee.)

Go, get my mask.

(He obeys, amid dead silence. Mrs. McFee mechanically surrenders mask to him. He returns. Opens door. Freda passes out. He follows.)

CURTAIN

ACT III—FREDA MOLOOF'S CABIN

Scene. *Freda Moloofs cabin. It is eleven forty-five at night. The room is large, and luxuriously furnished. Its walls are of logs stuffed between with brown moss. Doors of rough, unstained pine boards, also window-frames and sashes. Street door to rear, in centre. On either side of door is an ordinary, small-paned window. To left of door a plain chair. On rear wall, near door, are wooden pegs, from which hang cloaks, wraps, furs, etc., also wisp-brooms for brushing snow from moccasins.*

The luxury of furnishing is of the solid order. No gim-cracks, no bric-a-brac. Furniture is rough, made in the Klondike. Tables, chairs, etc., are unpolished; they are made from pine lumber, are unstained, rough, massive. There is no carpet. Bearskins, etc., litter the floor. Strange juxtaposition of rough pine furniture, costly rugs, etc.; and, strangest of all, a grand piano. The cheapest and simplest and ugliest of kerosene lamps are used for lighting purposes, also candles. On walls are magnificent moose-horns and other appropriate trophies and weapons of the Northland (such as great ivory-headed spears and a pair of tusks of the mammoth); but there are no framed paintings.

Midway between front and rear, and midway between centre and right, a large, wood-burning stove. Beside it a woodbox. On stove a tea-kettle is simmering. To left of stove, and near it, table, with table-cover on it, a few books and magazines, and a cheap kerosene lamp; around table several pine chairs. Between table and stove two easy chairs of rough pine, massive, thrown over with furs. On right, at front, against wall, a large, comfortable lounging-couch with many cushions. On left, at front, a grand piano. On piano a small, gilt French clock is ticking.

The room is luxurious, comfortable, picturesque, emphasizing the contact of civilization and the wilderness. In short, it is the best possible living apartment that money can purchase in the Klondike.

A Maid is in easy chair, reading magazine and yawning. Door opens on right. Indian enters with armful of firewood, which he carries to stove and dumps in woodbox. He proceeds to put several sticks of wood into stove and to adjust damper. His entrance arouses Maid, who looks up, yawns, lays magazine face-down on lap, yawns again, at same time stretching arms behind head, and glances at clock. It is quite a distance to clock. She rubs eyes and looks again.

MAID

Ten minutes to twelve. (Yawns.)

INDIAN

What time come?

MAID

(Shaking head.)

I don't know.

(Yawning.)

I never know.

INDIAN

Me go to bed.

MAID

You'd better not. She said we were to stay up.

INDIAN

What for? Much trouble you think? What she do? Where she go?

MAID

(Yawning.)

How should I know?

INDIAN

Sitka Charley take dogs. Sitka Charley big hurry. What for?

MAID

(Listening.)

There she comes now.

(Maid rises to her feet, like a soldier coming to attention, hastily puts magazine on table, and brushes down front of skirt. Indian puts another stick of wood into stove and busies himself with raking ashes level in ash-box of stove.)

(Street door opens. Freda enters, leading Vanderlip by the hand. Both are mittened and in same wraps, coats, etc., with which they left anteroom of Pioneer Hall.)

(Indian finishes with stove and goes out slowly to right. Maid goes to rear and helps Freda off with wraps, moccasins, etc.)

(Vanderlip, who has come in reluctantly, does not remove mittens or cap, and stands sullenly inside the door, though he cannot forbear glancing curiously around.)

FREDA

(Seeming in high spirits, while Maid is taking off her street moccasins.)

And now for a toddy! You've never tasted Minnie's. She makes them—

(Holding up hands.)

oh, to the king's taste, and to a Klondike king's at that.

VANDERLIP

(Brusquely.)

Sorry. Won't have time. What did you want me for?

FREDA

My! There's the man of it!

(Imitating his voice and manner.) What did you want me for?

(Natural voiced)

Can't let the poor woman catch her breath. Won't sit down for a moment in the warm.

(Motions to Maid to help him off with his bearskin overcoat.)

Must know what he's wanted for. Must know right away. Must go right away. Oh, my! Oh, my!

(Maid starts to help him off with overcoat. He jerks away from her.)

VANDERLIP

(Sullenly.)

What do you want to say to me? Fire away.

FREDA

(Laying hand on his arm.)

Floyd—

(Hesitating.)

—dear Floyd.... You are big and strong. I know, too, that you are kind. Be kind now, just a little kind, a very little. I can't talk with you here, this way. It would be ridiculous.

(Beginning to help him take off coat, in which operation his assistance is restricted to non-resistance.)

Come and sit by the fire a moment.

(Hands overcoat to Maid, who hangs it up on wall.)

Just for a moment.

(Untying ear-flaps, and removing his cap, which Maid hangs up. She pushes him on to chair and lifts one foot to remove street moccasins.)

VANDERLIP

(Helplessly expostulating.)

Now here, I say—

(She persists.)

I won't have a woman doing that for me.

(Pushes her away and removes moccasins himself. He stands up.)

I said I wasn't coming to your cabin, Freda; and I can't stay anyway—only for that one moment, that's all.

FREDA

(Taking his hand and starting to lead him forward.)

That is all I wanted, just the moment. And it is sweet of you to give it to me.

(Vanderlip pauses and looks around room with interest. Freda pauses with him. Maid remains in rear, putting moccasins away, etc.)

VANDERLIP

(More genially, forgetting to be sullen.)

I say, Freda, you're fixed comfortably.

FREDA

Think so?

VANDERLIP

It's grand style, I must say. Nothing like it in the land. You're the only person that has three rooms.

FREDA

Four—counting the kitchen.

VANDERLIP

And my cabin is one room.

FREDA

And you a millionaire.

VANDERLIP

But this is the Klondike—

FREDA

(Laughing and interrupting.)

Where even millionaires

(Imitating Dave Harney.) can't buy sweetenin' for their coffee an' mush. Dodgast the luck anyway.

(Vanderlip laughs appreciatively. They start on again to front, but he sees piano and stops again.)

VANDERLIP

If there ain't a piano! It cost you a pretty penny, I'll bet.

FREDA

(Leading him toward piano, half-singing, lightly.)

"You cannot pack a Broadwood half a mile." (Looking at him.)

Don't you know it?

(He shakes head.)

Don't know your Kipling!

(Sitting down at piano.)

Here's the way it goes—

(Plays and sings.)

"You couldn't pack a Broadwood half a mile,

You mustn't leave a fiddle in the damp,

You couldn't raft an organ up the Nile

And play it in an equatorial swamp "——

VANDERLIP

(Who had first gazed admiringly at her, then gazed curiously around until, by clock on piano, he sees what time it is, interrupting by bringing hand heavily down on keys of piano.)

I can't wait another second. What do you want with me?

FREDA

(Ceasing the song, looking up quite calmly, and placing hand over face of clock.)

I want you to stop looking at that clock. And

(Rising, taking him by hand, and leading him toward stove.)

I want you to come right over here and be good.

(Turning to Maid.)

Minnie.

(Maid, who has been waiting in rear, comes forward and again waits.)

(Freda pushes Vanderlip into easy chair near stove, runs to couch at right for cushion, which she puts behind his head, pressing his shoulders and head back upon it. She places fur-covered footstool under his feet. He has not relaxed himself, and in his stiff acceptance of comforts makes a ridiculous appearance.)

FREDA

(Giving cushion behind head a last pat.) And now you may smoke.

(Maid goes out to right.)

(Vanderlip rolls head back and forth on cushion. His hand searches for watch, which he draws forth from pocket. But before he can look at it Freda's hand covers the face of it.)

FREDA

Oh my! My! What a busy man it is!

(Maid enters with cigar-box on tray. Vanderlip takes a cigar, and while he examines it critically Freda puts watch back in his pocket.)

VANDERLIP

(Biting off end of cigar.)

Real Havana. And you can't buy them for love nor money. How do you manage it?

FREDA

(Striking match and holding it up to him.) Oh, I just do. I could have offered you worse, I assure you.

(Vanderlip puffs on cigar—long, slow, appreciative puffs. His face loses its sullen expression. He sighs contentedly. He relaxes his body, sinks back, and for the first time looks really comfortable.)

FREDA

And now, Minnie, you have your reputation to live up to.

MAID

(Hesitating an instant.)

The Scotch?

(Freda nods head, and Maid goes out to right.)

VANDERLIP

(Taking cigar from mouth and looking at it.)

I say, Freda, you can make a fellow comfortable.

FREDA

(Smiling.)

Think so?

VANDERLIP

(The sullenness returning into his face.) And you know how to make him uncomfortable.

FREDA

(Smiling.)

Think so?

VANDERLIP

You are, by long odds, the most brutal woman I ever met.

FREDA

(Incredulously and innocently aghast.) I?

VANDERLIP

(Harshly.)

I wouldn't treat a dog the way you treated me. (Growing angry.)

You treated me like a cur, the way you lugged me away from the dance.

FREDA

Think so?

VANDERLIP

I'd sooner a man beat me with a club, than take what I took from you. It was just as much as if you took a club to me. You beat me into submission, in front of everybody, until I followed at your heels—that's what you did.

FREDA

(With mock solemnity.)

141

Whom the Lord loveth he chasteneth.

VANDERLIP

But you are not the Lord. You are Freda—Freda

(Laughing and interrupting.)

And whom Freda chasteneth—

VANDERLIP

(Interrupting.)

She—

FREDA

(Interrupting.)

Not at all. The Lord is the Lord, but Freda is only a woman....

(A pause.)

VANDERLIP

(Impatiently.)

And?

FREDA

Her ways are different from the Lord's.

(She pulls her chair alongside of his, and rests one hand for a moment, caressingly, on his. Speaks softly.)

And aren't you glad?

(The caress has its effect. He is soothed, and puffs away at cigar with half-closed eyes.)

(Freda, unobserved, throws a swift glance at clock, listens intently as for sounds from without of an approaching sled, and betrays to her audience her anxiety and restlessness.)

(Maid enters with two glasses on a tray. Freda, observed by Vanderlip, sips from one glass, nods head approvingly, and passes it to him. Takes other glass herself.)

FREDA

Minnie. Candles.

(Maid moves about room, putting out lamps and lighting candles, which latter, with tissue-paper shades, shed softer light.)

(Vanderlip suddenly recollects himself and draws watch. Freda tries to cover watch with hand, but jails. Vanderlip sees watch and starts to rise from chair. Freda half rises and presses him back.)

VANDERLIP

(With note of real regret in his voice, glancing from cigar in one hand, and glass in other hand, to the stove, about the room, and then at Freda.)

It's a darn shame to leave all this, but I've really got to, Freda. I don't think I was ever so comfortable in my life.

FREDA

(Softly, almost whispering.)

Then why leave it, Floyd?

VANDERLIP

I've got to hit the trail to-night, right away. And I've got to get my trail clothes. That bearskin overcoat's too warm. Can't travel in it.

(Starts to rise.)

FREDA

(Pressing him back gently.)

Wait a minute. Let me think.

(Thinks a moment. Her face brightens.) Ah, the very thing. Why not send my Indian for your things? He can bring them here. That will give you a few minutes more of the warm—

VANDERLIP

(Interrupting, putting his arm out and around her waist.)

And of you, Freda.

(Freda lets his arm linger for a moment, then, warning him, by a look, of presence of Maid, gently disengages arm. Takes her time about disengaging it. Vanderlip sinks back comfortably on cushion.)

FREDA

(Turning to Maid.)

Minnie.

(Maid, who has finished lighting candles, approaches.)

Send Joe here. Tell him to put on his mittens and parka.

(Maid goes out to right.)

(Freda resumes seat, and lays one hand on Vanderlip's hand. Neither speaks.)

(Maid enters, followed by Indian, who, as he comes, is putting on parka and mittens.)

FREDA

You know Mr. Vanderlip's cabin?

INDIAN

(Nodding.)

Um.

FREDA

Give him the key, Floyd.

(Vanderlip reaches in pocket and gives key to Indian.)

You go Mr. Vanderlip's cabin and get parka—

VANDERLIP

(Interrupting.)

Dog-whip, fur cap, all together with parka.

FREDA

Dog-whip, fur cap, all together with parka. (Indian nods.)

VANDERLIP

And flask of whiskey on table.

FREDA

And flask of whiskey on table.

(Indian nods.)

VANDERLIP

And go quick.

FREDA

And go quick.

(Indian nods and starts toward door to rear. Makes exit. Freda rises, as though recollecting something.)

Excuse me, Floyd.

(Passes behind Vanderlip's back toward door to right, and unobserved beckons Maid. They pause at door to right.) Run quick, out the kitchen door, and catch Joe. Tell him not to come back. Tell him I said so—to go get drunk, anything, but not to come back.

(Vanderlip lifts heady turns head around, and is watching and listening.

Freda continues in slightly louder voice.)

And then, Cupid's stew.

(Maid makes exit to right.)

(Freda returns to chair, passing hand caressingly through Vanderlip's hair before she sits down.)

VANDERLIP

(Gruffly, suspiciously.)

What were you gassing about?

FREDA

(Mysteriously.)

Cupid's stew.

VANDERLIP

I heard it, but what is it?

FREDA

(Pausing and considering.)

Well, first you take the chafing-dish—

VANDERLIP

(Interrupting.)

What's the chafing-dish? Use them in churches, don't they? Burn incense in them, or something or other.

FREDA

(Laughing.)

A chafing-dish, silly, is a very pretty something you cook things in.

VANDERLIP

Oh, I see. A highfalutin' frying-pan.

FREDA

(Nodding.)

First you put some butter in it; and then, when the butter is melted, you stir in—oh, say a tablespoon of flour.

(Vanderlip is listening closely.)

When it is stirred smooth—

VANDERLIP

(Interrupting.)

Do you brown the flour?

FREDA

No, of course not.

VANDERLIP

(With comprehension.)

Oh.

FREDA

Then you stir in a cup of milk—Minnie's fixing it now, out in the kitchen—and in her case it will have to be condensed milk—

VANDERLIP

(Interrupting.)

St. Anthony's Cream's the best brand I know of.

(Regretfully.)

But you can't get it in this country.

FREDA

I've got some.

VANDERLIP

(In joyful amazement.)

No!

FREDA

(Nodding head.)

I have. Then you put in some boneless chicken—tinned—

VANDERLIP

(Interrupting.)

You got some of that, too?

FREDA

Yes. And then some mushrooms—tinned—

VANDERLIP

(Interrupting ecstatically.)

Freda, you're a wonder!

FREDA

Then season to taste,

(Rising to climax.) and there you are!

(Freda half rises, leaning toward him. He half rises to meet her, reaching for her with both arms, to put around her waist, but she catches his hands and very gently and slowly disengages herself. Her very manner of disengaging herself is caressing and seducing. They sink back slowly into their respective chairs.)

(Freda listens intently, as for the sound of a sled without. Glances anxiously at clock on piano. Vanderlip does not notice, for he is drawing his watch and looking at it.)

VANDERLIP

It's ten after twelve.

(Looks anxiously at door to right.)

Gee! I hate to go without having a crack at that Cupid's stew.

(He looks at Freda. She is gazing at him absently, apparently lost in meditation over him.)

Well?

FREDA

(Startled, as though discovered, in pretty embarrassment.)

Oh!

VANDERLIP

I was just wondering what you wanted to see me about.

(He draws his chair snugly against hers. She looks at him, studying him, as though trying to make up her mind to speak.) Well, what is it?

FREDA

(With steadiness and determination.)

Floyd, I am tired of the whole business. I want to go away—over the ice—anywhere—away. I can't live it out here till the river breaks next spring. I'll die. I know it. I want to quit it all and go away. And I want to go at once.

(She lays her hand in appeal on the back of his. His hand turns over and captures hers. He does not know what to say.)

Well?

VANDERLIP

(Hastily.)

I don't know what to say. Nothing I'd like better, Freda. You know that well enough.

(He presses her hand, and she nods.)

But you see I'm—

(Blurting it out.)

—I'm engaged. Of course you know that. Everybody knows it. The girl's coming in over the ice to marry me.

(Meditatively.)

Don't know what was up with me when I asked her, but it was a long while back, and I was all-fired young.

FREDA

And you intend to wait for her?

(He nods.)

And to marry her?

(He nods.)

Men sometimes make mistakes, you know, when they are young.

VANDERLIP

(Warmly.)

And this is one of them. What did I know about women then?

FREDA

(Slyly.)

Nothing to what you know about them now.

VANDERLIP

I should say so.

FREDA

But, Floyd, by persisting in the mistake, do you mend matters?

(He shakes his head dubiously.)

Will you be happy? Will she be happy? She is sure to find out the mistake, then it will be tragedy.

VANDERLIP

(In despair.)

I don't know. Women keep bothering me so. There are so many of them, and I like them all. Seems to me I like best the one I'm with at the time.

FREDA

Mrs. Eppingwell, let us say.

VANDERLIP

(With positiveness.)

Yes, Mrs. Eppingwell. Why, when I'm with her, I think there's nothing like her under the sun. I feel like going out and killing her husband just to get her.

FREDA

(Seductively.)

And when you are with me, Floyd?

(Vanderlip reaches out impulsively and draws her to him. Her head rests on his shoulder. She snuggles in to him in a contented way, her hand petting his. He buries his face in her hair. The scent of her hair gets into his brain and maddens him. He disengages hand from hers and slips it gradually up her bare arm. His other arm, about waist and shoulder, draws her closely against him. All the while, however, they are occupying their respective chairs. They remain this way for a long moment or so, his hand still progressing up her bare arm.)

151

FREDA

(Tearing herself suddenly loose from him and holding him from her at arms' length, tragically.)

Floyd! Floyd! I want to go away—out of the land—anywhere!—anywhere!

VANDERLIP

(Soothingly.)

Dear Freda.

FREDA

I am tired, tired, so tired of it all. I—I—

(Voice breaking.)

—I think I shall cry.

VANDERLIP

(Gently and soothingly drawing her to him.)

There, there, little woman. Brace up, buck up, don't give in.

FREDA

(Slowly disengaging herself and gently holding him off at arm's length.)

I've been running over in my mind the men I know, and reached the conclusion that... that...

VANDERLIP

(Beaming with self-complacency.)

I was the likeliest of the lot.

FREDA

(Quickly.)

No, not that, but... but... that I liked you best of all.

VANDERLIP

(Drawing her to him.)

Dear Freda.

FREDA

Dear Floyd.

(Door on right opens. They break away from each other and assume a more decorous position. Maid enters, bearing tray, on which are chafing-dish, dishes, napkins, etc., and a quart bottle of champagne. She sets tray on table. Freda serves Cupid's stew to Vanderlip, while Maid, a little to rear, is wrestling with champagne bottle.)

VANDERLIP

(Who has not noticed champagne bottle, aroused by popping of cork and turning around quickly, simulating a person roused from sleep, rubbing his eyes, etc.)

Wake me up, somebody. I'm dreaming. Pinch me.

(Takes hold of bottle, Maid still retaining her hold, and looks at it.)

The real thing.

(Releases bottle and looks admiringly at Freda.)

Freda, you're a peach. There isn't another bottle in the Klondike.

FREDA

Oh, yes, there is.

VANDERLIP

(Incredulously.)

You've got to show me.

FREDA

I've three dozen in the store-room—(Turning to Maid.)

Isn't that right, Minnie?

MAID

And two over. I counted them this afternoon.

VANDERLIP

(Awe-stricken.)

Gosh!

FREDA

All right, Minnie. You may go now.

(Maid goes out to right.)

(Vanderlip begins eating Cupid's stew. Shows that he is pleased with it. Freda watches him, herself eating. Glances at clock, and listens. She seems to hear something. Puts down her plate on table. A knock is heard on door at rear. Freda rises, goes swiftly to rear, and opens door.)

(An Indian enters. He is dazzled by the light, and pulls ice from lips. Freda shuts door. Vanderlip, after one glance around, goes on eating and drinking.)

INDIAN

Hello.

FREDA

(Not knowing his errand.) Hello.

INDIAN

Brrr! Much cold.

FREDA

Very cold.

INDIAN

Me come Sitka Charley.

FREDA

Oh, you are the man.

INDIAN

Sitka Charley say him come quick.

FREDA

How quick?

INDIAN

Maybe ten minutes. What time now?

FREDA

Fifteen minutes after twelve.

INDIAN

Him come twenty-five minutes after twelve. Ten minutes more him come, I think.

FREDA

How is the girl?

INDIAN

Much tired. Ride on sled. Plenty tired, cry little bit, like baby. She say must camp right away. Sitka Charley say make Dawson. She say no camp right away she die. Sitka Charley say don't care, make Dawson anyway. I go now. Good-by.

FREDA

Don't you want to go out in the kitchen and get warm?

INDIAN

No. Good-by.

FREDA

Good-by.

(Indian opens door and goes out.)

(Freda returns to chair at stove.)

(Freda Sitting down.)

You haven't told me how you like it.

VANDERLIP

(Turning plate upside down.) Actions speak louder than words. (She helps him to some more.) Let me see, Cupid's slumgullion, eh?

FREDA

(Laughing.)

Cupid's stew.

VANDERLIP

(Thrusting fork into stew on his plate.) What's in a name, so long as it's in your plate anyway?

(Eats silently jor a space.)

FREDA

(Softly.)

Floyd.

(He is absorbed in eating.)

Floyd.

VANDERLIP

(Looking at her.) Unh-hunh.

FREDA

(Still softly.)

I've been thinking. Why couldn't we go down river?

VANDERLIP

(Dropping fork and looking at her blankly, then around room, then at plate, and holding up glass of champagne—pathetically.)

And leave all this?

FREDA

Why not? We'd soon be down in the world, where we could swim in wine and all kinds of good things.

VANDERLIP

(Seriously.)

I don't know, Freda. I almost believe you've got to be in a place like this to get the value out of things. I tell you champagne on tap is not all it's cracked up to be. It never bites in and lays hold the way this does. Down in the world it's all wine and no thirst—

FREDA

(Interrupting.)

And up here it's all thirst and no wine.

VANDERLIP

(Enthusiastically.)

But when you do get hold of the wine—Lord! Lord!

(Tilts hack head and empties glass, his face beaming like to the full moon. He regards Freda thoughtfully as she fills his glass, and speaks with sudden suspicion.) You don't happen to care for palaces, do you?

FREDA

(Shaking her head.)

Why, what put that into your head?

VANDERLIP

Well, I had a hankering after them myself, till I got to thinking a while back, and I've about sized it up that one gets fat living in palaces, and soft and lazy. No sir, no champagne on tap and soft summer skies for me.

FREDA

I suppose it's nice in palaces—for a time. But one would soon tire. The world is good, but life should be many-sided. The way we'll do it will be to rough and knock about for a while, and then rest up somewhere.

(Vanderlip begins to lean forward, interested.)

Off to the South Seas on a yacht, then, say a nibble of Paris.

VANDERLIP

(Gleefully.)

Paris!

FREDA

Then a winter in South America, and a summer in Norway—

VANDERLIP

(Interrupting.)

I always wanted a look-see, at South America.

FREDA

A few months in England—

VANDERLIP

(Interrupting.)

Good society?

FREDA

Certainly. And then, heigho! for the dogs and the sleds and the Hudson Bay Country!

VANDERLIP

(Half rising, enthusiastically.)

Freda, you were made for me! It's just the life I want. I couldn't have hit it off better myself if I'd tried. The way you put it—a bit of this, and a bit of that—variety, you know—that's me.

FREDA

That's it, variety, change. A strong man like you, full of vitality and go, could not possibly stand a palace for a year.

(He shakes his head.)

It's all very well for effeminate men, but you weren't made for such a life. You are masculine, intensely masculine.

VANDERLIP

(Taking her hand and beginning to draw her toward him.)

Do you think so?

FREDA

(Yielding herself.)

It doesn't require thinking. I know. Have you ever noticed that it was easy to make women care for you?

VANDERLIP

(Superbly innocent, yet showing by his expression that he agrees with

25

her.)

Oh, I don't know.

FREDA

You know it is so.

VANDERLIP

Well, for the sake of argument, yes.

FREDA

It is very easy. And why?

VANDERLIP

(Still playing innocent.)

Darned if I know.

FREDA

(Impressively.)

Because you are masculine. You strike the deepest chords of a woman's heart. Woman is weak. You are a wall of strength to her. You are something to cling to—big-muscled, strong, and brave. In short, because you are a man.

(He folds her to him.)

Dear, dear Floyd!

(She lies in his arms a long moment, both still on their respective chairs. Then she slowly and gently disengages herself, at the same time stealing a glance at the clock.)

VANDERLIP

(Holding up her arm and studying it for a moment.)

How much do you weigh, Freda?

FREDA

(Smiling.)

What now?

VANDERLIP

I just wanted to know.

FREDA

But why?

VANDERLIP

Oh, nothing, I was just thinking you were not the kind to put on fat?

FREDA

(Decisively.) Well, I think not!

VANDERLIP

(Suddenly, by her hands, lifts her to her feet and thrusts her several steps away from him, then, sinking back in chair and running his eyes critically over her) Your lines are good.

FREDA

(Lightly)

Think so?

VANDERLIP

You just bet I do.

(Jubilantly)

You'll never get fat!

FREDA

(Coming to his chair and rumpling his hair.)

No, thank goodness, I wasn't born that way.

VANDERLIP

(Beginning pompously)

Now some women—

FREDA

(Interrupting)

The Lisznayi, for example.

VANDERLIP

(Spontaneously, positively.)

She'll never get fat, Freda.

FREDA

Oh, she won't, eh? How do you know? You'd never have guessed it all of yourself. She must have told you.

(Vanderlip shows confusion.)

Why, she's started already. She's carrying twenty pounds more than she ought. It spoils her figure. And—my!—now that she's started, won't she just put it on!

VANDERLIP

(Anxiously.)

But how do you know?

FREDA

I've my eyes. So have you. Surely you've noticed it?

VANDERLIP

(Slowly.)

Honest, now, I've had my suspicions that way. (He remains silent for a moment or so. Freda rumples his hair.)

I like that.

FREDA

What?

VANDERLIP

That what you are doing.

FREDA

Oh!

(Slaps his arm playfully, and sits down in her chair. Listens intently for sounds from without, while Vanderlip sips from glass.)

VANDERLIP

(After a pause, setting down glass and looking amorously at Freda.)

Say, Freda, do you know...

(A pause. Freda glances at clock.)

Do you know what I'd like?

FREDA

Not in the slightest.

VANDERLIP

Well, I'll tell you. I'd like to see you with your hair down.

FREDA

(Change in whole manner beginning here, but beginning slightly.)

Think so?

VANDERLIP

You just bet I would.

FREDA

(Rising.)

Wait a moment.

(Passes behind him to door at right.)

(Vanderlip rests under the idea that she has gone to take down hair, fills glass, and leans complacently back in chair and sips from glass.)

(Freda opens door to right and beckons. Closes door, listens for a moment on way back to chair, and sits down.)

VANDERLIP

(Looking at her hair, still up, surprised and grieved.)

Why, I thought all the time you were taking it down.

(Freda laughs her silvery, scornful laughter. Vanderlip is puzzled, thinks she is teasing him.)

(Maid enters, unobserved by Vanderlip. Freda issues her order with her eyes, glancing at Vanderlip's bearskin overcoat hanging on wall to rear. Maid goes and gets coat and returns, still unobserved by Vanderlip, at the rear of whom she stands waiting.)

VANDERLIP

(Expostulating.)

Now I say, Freda.

(Freda still laughs.)

What's the matter anyway?

FREDA

I have just recollected.

VANDERLIP

(Puzzled.)

What?

FREDA

That you had an engagement at twelve sharp.

VANDERLIP

I did. But it will keep.

FREDA

It is now half-past twelve.

VANDERLIP

Well, and what of it?

FREDA

Nothing, only...

(Pauses and considers.)

VANDERLIP

Only what?

FREDA

Only, isn't it rather cold down at the water-hole?

(Vanderlip is stunned jor a moment, and can only stare at her in a bewildered way.)

(Her laughter, at his bewilderment, becomes wholly mirthful.)

Minnie, help Mr. Vanderlip on with his overcoat.

(Vanderlip glances swiftly around and sees Maid holding coat. He looks at his watch very slowly, and puts it away very slowly. Slowly empties glass of champagne, and carefully puts empty glass on table. Just as slowly drags

165

himself out of chair and to his feet. Maid offers to help on with overcoat, but he ignores her.)

FREDA

(Who has ceased laughing, showing that she is a bit frightened by his preternatural calmness, but still keeping her nerve.)

Let me thank you for your kindness, Floyd. I wanted half an hour or so of your time, and you have given it. The turning to the left, as you leave the cabin, leads quickest to the water-hole. Good-night. I'm going to bed.

(Starts to go toward door at left.)

Minnie, see Mr. Vanderlip out, please.

(Turning head over shoulder, looking back at Vanderlip, and beginning again her silvery laughter. Vanderlip has not spoken a word. He springs, lionlike, after her, seizing her by the arm and whirling her fiercely about, face to face, and still keeping his clutch.)

Don't be rough.

(He glares at her. She still keeps her nerve, speaks lightly.)

On second thought—

(Looks at his detaining hand.)

—I've decided not to go to bed. Don't be ridiculous, Floyd.

(He growls inarticulately.)

Tragedy doesn't at all become you. Do sit down and be comfortable.

(To Maid, who has remained composed and holding coat.)

Mr. Vanderlip doesn't want his coat yet awhile. (Maid goes to rear, hangs up coat, and remains at rear, waiting.)

VANDERLIP

(Speaking with slow, clear enunciation.) What do you know about the water-hole?

(Freda laughs. He closes his grip on her arm till she winces.)

What do you know about the water-hole?

FREDA

(Lightly.)

More than you know.

VANDERLIP

(Again closing grip.)

Then tell me. I want to know.

FREDA

(Wincing, but still lightly.)

I know that the fair lady waiting there has flown away a good half-hour ago.

VANDERLIP

Where?

FREDA

Down the river.

VANDERLIP

How do you know it?

FREDA

I arranged it.

VANDERLIP

(Softening for a moment.)

Tell me, it was because you wanted me?

167

FREDA

(Defiantly.)

No.

VANDERLIP

(Hardening again.) Then you didn't want me? (She shakes her head.)

You don't want me?

(She shakes head.)

Well, then, will you have me?—Now? (She shakes head.)

Then this was a game you worked on me?

FREDA

Yes.

VANDERLIP

You didn't mean a word of it?

FREDA

Not a word of it. I was playing.

VANDERLIP

(Grimly.)

Well, I wasn't, that's the difference.

FREDA

Do let go of my arm. You are hurting me.

VANDERLIP

(Ignoring her protest, dragging her roughly by her arm to the front and just to left of table, holding her face to face with him, and beginning to speak faster.)

Look here, Freda, I'm a fool. I know it. I was a fool there in that chair. You put it all over me. You women all make a fool of me. I don't think quick. I'm not used to it, I guess. My tongue is awkward. I can't think of bright things to say, or the right things to say. And I believe what is said to me. And then I like women, too. I can't help it. I was born that way. I just like them, and they take advantage of me—

FREDA

(Interrupting.)

Won't you let go of me and sit down?

VANDERLIP

(Ignoring her.)

Why do they take advantage of me?

(Freda shrugs her shoulders.)

Because I am a fool. Because I am playing their game and don't know how to play it. They know how to play it. They ought to know—it is their game. A man's a fool to buck another man's game. The percentage is all in favor of the house. And a man is a bigger fool to buck a woman's game. And I've been dead soft and easy. I know it. I've played your game and you've tied knots in me...

(He pauses, as though debating the next thing to say.)

FREDA

(Lightly.)

I must say you are untying the knots fast.

VANDERLIP

(With touch of anger.)

I'm untying nothing. I'm going to begin tying. What I'm going to do is to play my game, and you're going to play it with me, my lady.

(His speech grows slow and clear again.) Do you know what my game is?

(Freda shakes her head.)

It's not palavering, and being society-monkey, and ducking, and bowing, and scraping, and giving crooked talk, and saying smart things, and that sort of stuff. It's just this—

(He takes hold of her other arm with other hand, and puts the pressure on with both hands. At first she merely winces but he grips until she cries aloud in pain. Maid shows alarm for first time, and starts hastily forward.)

That's it. Muscle's my game—the only game I can play, and I've been a fool to go out of my class.

MAID

(Interrupting, to Freda.)

What shall I do?

FREDA

Nothing. It is all right.

MAID

Shall I go for help?

FREDA

No, no.

(To Vanderlip.)

Let go of me, Floyd. You are crushing my arms.

VANDERLIP

(Laughing savagely.)

Did you let go when you crushed me?

FREDA

(With blaze of defiance.)

You coward!

VANDERLIP

(Savagely.)

Were you less coward when you beat me down to my knees with your woman's wit, your woman's beauty, your woman's weapons? Your face is beautiful. Your body is beautiful. With these have you drawn me to you, making yourself soft and yielding, so that at a distance the very feel of you was soft and yielding—

(With scorn.)

—a play actress, you! Your mind is quick. Your tongue is crooked. You lied to me. When you let me hold your hand, you lied to me. When you looked softly at me, or passed your hand through my hair, you lied to me. When you came against me and rested your head on my breast so that the scent of your hair got into my brain and maddened me, you lied to me. You knew all the time that my blood was pounding up hot within me, you knew all the time that I was honest and playing fair, and all the time you were lying to me.

(He pauses and debates upon what next to say.)

MAID

(Calmly, to Freda.)

Shall I go for help?

VANDERLIP

(Ferociously.)

Shut up, you!

(Continuing, to Freda.)

Well, I've taken your medicine. Now you take mine. Here it is. I want you. I'm pretty sure I'd sooner have you than Loraine. You can marry me if you want, but marry or no marry, you're mine. Down river you go with me tonight, my lady, so you'd better tell that girl of yours to pack your duds.

FREDA

(Laughing defiantly in his face.)

Think so?

VANDERLIP

(Maddened by desire of her.)

I know so—and here's a foretaste of my game. Tell me how you like it.

(Bends her back, face upturned, gets proper grips so that she is helpless, and deliberately and passionately kisses her several times on the lips. Maid springs upon him, but he flings her off and away with one arm. Holds Freda by one arm again.)

How do you like it, eh? How do you like it?

FREDA

(Almost suffocating with rage, wiping lips with back of free hand.)

You beast! You beast! You beast!

(Maid is starting to spring at him again.) No, no, Minnie! Stop! I can deal with him.

VANDERLIP

Not in a man's game, Freda.

FREDA

(All defiance.)

In a man's game, Floyd Vanderlip.

(She no longer winces nor struggles to free herself, but confronts him,

172

head erect, expression of cold anger on face.)

VANDERLIP

(Looking at her admiringly for a moment.) Ah, you beauty! You've made me mad for you. I'll crush you into submission as you crushed me into submission at the dance to-night. You beat me down to my knees, but I'll bring you down on your knees to me till you're glad to kiss the toe of my moccasin.

(He surveys her again.)

And now, you beauty, you beauty, I am thirsty for your lips again.

(He starts to bend her back again, but she revises to struggle, holding her face up to him defiantly. He pauses.)

Well, why don't you fight and scratch and claw around some?

FREDA

Because I won't give you the chance to pull and haul and maul me around, that is all.

VANDERLIP

(Who, as usual, is baffled by a change of attitude.)

Then I'll kiss you.

FREDA

You may pollute me with your lips, but you shall not master me with your strength.

VANDERLIP

(Gaily.)

Nay, nay, not pollute. You should call it (Imitating Mrs. McFee.) "contameenate." That's right. Blaze away at me with those eyes of yours. You may keep quiet with your body, but you can't take the fight out of your eyes.

I tell you that blaze gives value to your kisses, and now I'm going to—

(Leans forward to kiss her, while she remains motionless and passive. He pauses, with lips close to hers.)

Nothing like prolonging anticipation, eh? You know you said I was masculine, intensely masculine. How do you like it? How do you like leaning up against the wall of my strength? Ah, you beauty! You beauty!

FREDA

(Suddenly listening.)

Minnie! Open the door!

(A jingling of dog bells is heard without, and a man's voice crying "Haw!" Maid runs toward the door. Vanderlip listens, still holding Freda close in his arms. A knock at door. Maid throws open door.)

FREDA

(In triumphant voice, as door is thrown open.)

Now will you let go of me?

(Enter Mrs. Eppingwell, followed by Capt. Eppingwell and a Northwest mounted Policeman.)

(Mrs. Eppingwell, looking at Policeman, points at Vanderlip.)

(Policeman hesitates, embarrassed at interrupting such a scene.)

(Vanderlip and Freda in consternation, he still holding her. He releases her abruptly and is himself all awkwardness and confusion. Freda separates from him, moving away unconsciously several steps, her eyes fixed upon Mrs. Eppingwell.)

FREDA

(Surprise, awe, etc.)

You!

MRS. EPPINGWELL

(Sharp and businesslike.)

Yes, I. And I am glad I am not too late.

FREDA

(Striving to recover her poise, speaking automatically in artificial manner.)

Delighted, I assure you.

(With sudden break in manner, becoming candid.)

No, I am not delighted at all.

MRS. EPPINGWELL

I should scarcely think so.

FREDA

It is intrusion.

MRS. EPPINGWELL

It is intrusion, I know, but—

FREDA

(Interrupting, again artificial manner.) Oh, not at all.

(Starting toward Mrs. Eppingwell.) Won't you take off your wraps?

(To Maid.)

Minnie!

(Maid offers to help Mrs. Eppingwell off with wraps.)

MRS. EPPINGWELL

(Declining Maid's offer.)

No, it is not necessary. We shall stop only a moment.

FREDA

(Artificial manner.)

I hope you'll pardon my curiosity, but—(Hesitates an instant.) —why didn't you come sooner? What was the delay?

MRS. EPPINGWELL

(Indicating Policeman, who bows.)

I had to get this gentleman. It took time—

POLICEMAN

(Interrupting, bowing.)

Sorry.

MRS. EPPINGWELL

And then I went to the wrong water-hole.

(Freda and Vanderlip both start, Mrs. Eppingwell observing Vanderlip's start.)

Good morning, Mr. Vanderlip.

VANDERLIP

(Awkwardly.)

Hum, yes. How do you do? Good morning.

FREDA

(The real state of affairs dawning on her.) I see. You expected to find me at the water-hole.

(Mrs. Eppingwell nods.)

And you didn't.

MRS. EPPINGWELL

No. Then I went to the other water-hole.

FREDA

Expecting to find me?

MRS. EPPINGWELL

Yes. Then I came here.

FREDA

(With mock admiration.)

Unerring instinct.

MRS. EPPINGWELL

(Replying in kind.)

Yes, wasn't it?

FREDA

Er—by the way, didn't you find anybody at the second water-hole?

MRS. EPPINGWELL

A strange woman. I thought she was you at first. She seemed restless enough.

VANDERLIP

(Starts at mention of strange woman, suddenly moving toward the street door.)

I've fooled around here long enough. I'm going.

FREDA

Good luck, Floyd.

POLICEMAN

(Stepping forward, meeting and stopping Vanderlip.)

Sorry.

VANDERLIP

(Irritated.)

What's the matter now?

POLICEMAN

(Drawing document from pocket.)

I've got a warrant for you. Forgery. Sorry.

VANDERLIP

(Astounded.)

What in hell—

(Breaks off.)

POLICEMAN

Sorry.

VANDERLIP

(Expostulating.)

Now look here, I say, whose game is this?

(Freda laughs her silvery laughter, it is laughter of amusement only.)

FREDA

(To Mrs. Eppingwell, still laughing, accusingly.)

You did this.

MRS. EPPINGWELL

(Nodding.)

I had tried everything else to stop him from running away.

FREDA

(Laughing merrily and shaking her head.) Poor Floyd! Poor, poor Floyd!

VANDERLIP

(Wrathfully.)

Look here, Mrs. Eppingwell. This is your work. You'd better call it off. I'm done with bucking other people's games.

(Starts toward door, but Policeman lays hand on his arm.)

Get out of my way, you whipper-snapper!

POLICEMAN

(Not backing down a bit.)

Sorry.

VANDERLIP

(Flinging off hand, but remaining where he is.)

You'd better call him off, Mrs. Eppingwell, or there'll be the almightiest ruction round here you ever saw.

FREDA

(Lightly.)

Don't be in a hurry, Floyd. She's gone.

VANDERLIP

No, she isn't.

FREDA

Ask Mrs. Eppingwell.

MRS. EPPINGWELL

Whom do you mean?

FREDA

The strange, restless lady at the water-hole.

MRS. EPPINGWELL

Why, yes. She went away on a sled down the river.

VANDERLIP

Who'd she go with?

MRS. EPPINGWELL

With nobody. She had an Indian dog-driver, though.

(Vanderlip makes gesture of despair, signifying that he has been completely beaten. Freda laughs merrily.)

VANDERLIP

(Wrathfully.)

Oh, you women!

MRS. EPPINGWELL

(To Freda.)

Who is this strange lady?

FREDA

(Indicating Vanderlip.)

Ask him.

(Mrs. Eppingwell looks inquiringly at Vanderlip.)

VANDERLIP

(Wrathfully.)

None of your business, you and your games! I quit. I've bucked myself broke against you—(Whirling on Freda.)—against all of you.

(To Policeman.)

Go ahead, arrest me. It's a fake, and you know it. But go ahead.

POLICEMAN

I've only got my orders. Sorry. You'll come along peaceably?

(Vanderlip grunts savage assent.)

VANDERLIP

You know it's a fake.

POLICEMAN

I know only my orders. Sorry.

(General movement of preparation to leave.)

FREDA

(To Mrs. Eppingwell.)

It's too bad you can't stop longer, but—

(Suddenly breaks off and listens intently.)

(A jingling oj dog bells is heard without, and shouts of men. A knock on street door. Maid opens door. Flossie appears in doorway and enters. Sitka Charley enters at her heels and closes door. Flossie is dazzled by the lights and looks about hesitatingly. She is well frosted up. A nose-strap is across her nose. She removes nose-strap. Looks about, and sees Vanderlip. Freda starts toward her, impulsively, to receive her.)

FLOSSIE

(Making a weak little lame run toward Vanderlip, with infinite relief in her voice.)

Floyd!

VANDERLIP

(Dazed.)

Flossie!

(He opens his arms and she staggers and falls into them. Her head lies on his breast for a space, while he holds her and stares helplessly around. Then she lifts her head, inviting the kiss, and perforce he bends head and kisses her.)

FLOSSIE

(Infinite gladness.)

Oh, Floyd! Floyd!

VANDERLIP

Dear, dear Flossie!

FLOSSIE

(Still in his arms, but throwing her head back to look at him, in playful manner.)

You big, impatient man!

(Vanderlip is puzzled, and only awkwardly pats her shoulder with one arm that is around her.)

You cruel, cruel man!

(He is still puzzled.)

Couldn't wait. Couldn't let me have my night's rest and arrive in the morning fresh.

VANDERLIP

Ah—hum—yes.

(She puts her lips up to him and he again kisses her.)

(Sitka Charley remains inside street door. Capt. Eppingwell is restless, betraying a feeling that it is time to go. Policeman is restless. Mrs. Eppingwell and Freda, now near to each other, are looking on.)

FLOSSIE

My! What lots of dogs you must have!

VANDERLIP

(More puzzled than ever.)

Hum, yes.

FLOSSIE

First came an Indian with six dogs. You know, the Indian with one eye.

(Mrs. Eppingwell and Capt. Eppingwell look at each other significantly. Vanderlip, after a moment's hesitancy, nods.)

Then came the second Indian with eight dogs.

(Mrs. Eppingwell looks inquiringly at Capt. Eppingwell, who shakes head, then each looks bepuzzlement at the other. Vanderlip, again hesitating, nods.)

And then came Sitka Charley with seven of the most magnificent dogs I ever saw. Oh, Floyd, they were just grand!

(Mrs. Eppingwell and Capt. Eppingwell look more bepuzzled than ever. Vanderlip looks across at Freda with comprehension, by his look as much as saying, "You are responsible for this." Freda smiles. Mrs. Eppingwell and Capt. Eppingwell observe the proceeding, and look at each other significantly.) We just flew along—like the wind!

VANDERLIP

(Seeing the whole situation and lying up to it.)

I just bet you did. I knew they'd bring you in on the jump. I told them I didn't want any loafing, and... well, from the looks of it, I guess there wasn't any.

FLOSSIE

(Snuggling in against him.)

Couldn't wait a bit longer, could you, dear?

VANDERLIP

(Holding her closely.)

You just bet I couldn't.

POLICEMAN

(Unobserved by Flossie, whose back is toward him, stepping forward toward Vanderlip, the warrant still in his hand.).

Sorry—

MRS. EPPINGWELL

(Interrupting, stepping toward him.)

Give it to me.

(Policeman hands warrant to her.)

It will be all right. You understand.

POLICEMAN

(Nodding, pulling on mittens, and bowing very politely.)

Then I will wish you good night.

(Makes exit with final bow.)

CAPT. EPPINGWELL

(To Mrs. Eppingwell, indicating desire to go.)

We're scarcely needed here, I think.

MRS. EPPINGWELL

One moment, Archie. I'm all in a daze, and I'm curious.

(Turning to Sitka Charley.)

Charley, the team of dogs you drove, whose were they?

FREDA

(Who, now that the fight is over and won, is on the verge of breaking down, interrupts Sitka Charley, and speaks herself.)

Now I wish you would all go home and leave me alone. I want to go to bed.

MRS. EPPINGWELL

(Gently.)

But I am curious, Freda, as you were curious. I want to know. I insist.

FREDA

(Choking, on the verge of tears.)

Please, please go.

FLOSSIE

(Who has lifted head and been regarding Freda, to Vanderlip. Loud enough for all to hear, but not too loud.)

Who is that woman?

VANDERLIP

(Painfully embarrassed, hesitatingly.)

Well... you see, Flossie... it's like this.

FLOSSIE

(With asperity.)

She is not a friend of yours?

VANDERLIP

No, no, of course not. You see, this is the Klondike. Things are different here than from what you've been used to, and... and...

FLOSSIE

(Interrupting, showing in voice and demeanor comprehension of Freda's status.)

Oh, I understand. It will be better for us to go, I think.

(They start toward street door, Vanderlip supporting Flossie around waist. She is very tired and leans heavily against him. He puts on bearskin coat, mittens, etc. He does not speak, though he nods awkwardly. As they make exit he glances back at Freda.)

FREDA

(To Mrs. Eppingwell, harshly.)

Now will you go.

MRS. EPPINGWELL

(Gently.)

No, I insist. There has been a misunderstanding.

(Freda, tears imminent, makes nervous exclamation, and with both hands makes nervous gesture. Turns her back, walks rapidly to front, and throws herself into easy chair, where she sits, face up, facing audience.)

MRS. EPPINGWELL

(To Sitka Charley.)

Those dogs you drove, Charley. Whose were they?

SITKA CHARLEY

(Hesitating, shifting weight from one leg to the other and back again, looking appealingly at back of chair in which Freda is seated.)

Me no know.

MRS. EPPINGWELL

(Impatiently.)

Of course you know.

SITKA CHARLEY

(Still hesitatingly, still shifting weight back and forth, still looking appealingly at back of chair occupied by Freda.)

Maybe know, maybe not know.

MRS. EPPINGWELL

(Imperatively.)

Tell me.

SITKA CHARLEY

(Angrily.)

What for, all you womans? Make Sitka Charley much tired. All the time,

(Imitating their manner.)

"Charley, tell me this, Charley, tell me that." All the time, "Charley, no tell this, Charley, no tell that." Sitka Charley tired. Sitka Charley much tired. Sitka Charley dam tired. Now Sitka Charley tell.

(He pauses, while Mrs. Eppingwell waits expectantly, and Freda, with expressionless face, faces audience.)

Sitka Charley big fool, too. Him think you love Vanderlip. Him think Freda love Vanderlip. (Shaking head.)

No love. All the same make Vanderlip big fool. All the time all womans make all mans big fool. You say, No tell Freda. Freda say, No tell you. All right. Sitka Charley no tell. Now Sitka Charley much tired. Now him tell. Um, him drive Freda's dogs. Freda say, "Charley, bring Flossie girl much quick."

(Looking at Mrs. Eppingwell with expression of pride, boastfully.)

Sitka Charley bring Flossie girl much quick.

MRS. EPPINGWELL

Who was the woman at the water-hole?

SITKA CHARLEY

Um Lisznayi woman.

(Mrs. Eppingwell is surprised. Capt. Eppingwell makes dumb show of delight.)

MRS. EPPINGWELL

(Beaten, pathetically.)

Archie, will you ever have faith in me again?

SITKA CHARLEY

(Moving toward door, turning toward back of Freda's chair.)

Dogs much hungry.

(Stops and waits, looking at Freda's chair.)

Um, me go feed dogs.

(After regarding chair for a moment, starts on toward street door. Again stops and looks at chair.)

I go now, Freda.

FREDA

(Not turning head, expressionless face and voice.)

Good night, Charley.

(Sitka Charley makes exit. Door slams.)

(Mrs. Eppingwell looks toward Freda's chair, starts as though to go to Freda, hesitates, and stops. Turns upon Capt. Eppingwell and shoves him toward street door. Capt. Eppingwell makes exit. Door slams. Mrs. Eppingwell remains standing on one side of door, looking toward Freda's chair. Maid stands on other side of door, looking at Mrs. Eppingwell.)

(When door slams, Freda rises to her feet. The breakdown has come.)

FREDA

Thank God!

(Without looking toward street door, or becoming aware that Mrs. Eppingwell still remains, Freda goes rapidly to right, to couch, sobs struggling up, her breast heaving. She sinks to floor, resting arms on couch, face buried in arms and couch, and sobs convulsively.)

(Mrs. Eppingwell comes forward and touches Freda on shoulder.)

FREDA

(Starting, but not looking up.)

It is all right, Minnie. You may go to bed.

(Goes on sobbing.)

(Mrs. Eppingwell waits a moment, sits down on couch, and rests hand on Freda's head.)

MRS. EPPINGWELL

(Very gently.)

Freda.

FREDA

(Starting with violent surprise and looking up.)

You!

MRS. EPPINGWELL

(Gently.)

Yes, I.

FREDA

(Trying to be harsh, but succeeding in being only reproachful.)

I asked you to go.

(Turns face away from Mrs. Eppingwell and looks straight forward toward audience.)

MRS. EPPINGWELL

(Gently.)

Freda

(Freda turns head and looks into Mrs. Eppingwell's face. Mrs. Eppingwell puts her arm around Freda's shoulder and draws her close. Freda bursts into tears and buries face in Mrs. Eppingwell's lap. Mrs. Eppingwell bends over her, soothing her.)

CURTAIN

About Author

Family

Jack London's mother, Flora Wellman, was the fifth and youngest child of Pennsylvania Canal builder Marshall Wellman and his first wife, Eleanor Garrett Jones. Marshall Wellman was descended from Thomas Wellman, an early Puritan settler in the Massachusetts Bay Colony. Flora left Ohio and moved to the Pacific coast when her father remarried after her mother died. In San Francisco, Flora worked as a music teacher and spiritualist, claiming to channel the spirit of a Sauk chief, Black Hawk.

Biographer Clarice Stasz and others believe London's father was astrologer William Chaney. Flora Wellman was living with Chaney in San Francisco when she became pregnant. Whether Wellman and Chaney were legally married is unknown. Most San Francisco civil records were destroyed by the extensive fires that followed the 1906 earthquake; nobody knows what name appeared on her son's birth certificate. Stasz notes that in his memoirs, Chaney refers to London's mother Flora Wellman as having been his "wife"; he also cites an advertisement in which Flora called herself "Florence Wellman Chaney".

According to Flora Wellman's account, as recorded in the San Francisco Chronicle of June 4, 1875, Chaney demanded that she have an abortion. When she refused, he disclaimed responsibility for the child. In desperation, she shot herself. She was not seriously wounded, but she was temporarily deranged. After giving birth, Flora turned the baby over for care to Virginia Prentiss, an African-American woman and former slave. She was a major maternal figure throughout London's life. Late in 1876, Flora Wellman married John London, a partially disabled Civil War veteran, and brought her baby John, later known as Jack, to live with the newly married couple. The family moved around the San Francisco Bay Area before settling in Oakland, where London completed public grade school.

In 1897, when he was 21 and a student at the University of California,

Berkeley, London searched for and read the newspaper accounts of his mother's suicide attempt and the name of his biological father. He wrote to William Chaney, then living in Chicago. Chaney responded that he could not be London's father because he was impotent; he casually asserted that London's mother had relations with other men and averred that she had slandered him when she said he insisted on an abortion. Chaney concluded by saying that he was more to be pitied than London. London was devastated by his father's letter; in the months following, he quit school at Berkeley and went to the Klondike during the gold rush boom.

Early life

London was born near Third and Brannan Streets in San Francisco. The house burned down in the fire after the 1906 San Francisco earthquake; the California Historical Society placed a plaque at the site in 1953. Although the family was working class, it was not as impoverished as London's later accounts claimed. London was largely self-educated.

In 1885, London found and read Ouida's long Victorian novel Signa. He credited this as the seed of his literary success. In 1886, he went to the Oakland Public Library and found a sympathetic librarian, Ina Coolbrith, who encouraged his learning. (She later became California's first poet laureate and an important figure in the San Francisco literary community).

In 1889, London began working 12 to 18 hours a day at Hickmott's Cannery. Seeking a way out, he borrowed money from his foster mother Virginia Prentiss, bought the sloop Razzle-Dazzle from an oyster pirate named French Frank, and became an oyster pirate himself. In his memoir, John Barleycorn, he claims also to have stolen French Frank's mistress Mamie. After a few months, his sloop became damaged beyond repair. London hired on as a member of the California Fish Patrol.

In 1893, he signed on to the sealing schooner Sophie Sutherland, bound for the coast of Japan. When he returned, the country was in the grip of the panic of '93 and Oakland was swept by labor unrest. After grueling jobs in a jute mill and a street-railway power plant, London joined Coxey's Army and began his career as a tramp. In 1894, he spent 30 days for vagrancy in the Erie County Penitentiary at Buffalo, New York. In The Road, he wrote:

Man-handling was merely one of the very minor unprintable horrors of the Erie County Pen. I say 'unprintable'; and in justice I must also say undescribable. They were unthinkable to me until I saw them, and I was no spring chicken in the ways of the world and the awful abysses of human degradation. It would take a deep plummet to reach bottom in the Erie County Pen, and I do but skim lightly and facetiously the surface of things as I there saw them.

After many experiences as a hobo and a sailor, he returned to Oakland and attended Oakland High School. He contributed a number of articles to the high school's magazine, The Aegis. His first published work was "Typhoon off the Coast of Japan", an account of his sailing experiences.

As a schoolboy, London often studied at Heinold's First and Last Chance Saloon, a port-side bar in Oakland. At 17, he confessed to the bar's owner, John Heinold, his desire to attend university and pursue a career as a writer. Heinold lent London tuition money to attend college.

London desperately wanted to attend the University of California, Berkeley. In 1896, after a summer of intense studying to pass certification exams, he was admitted. Financial circumstances forced him to leave in 1897 and he never graduated. No evidence suggests that London wrote for student publications while studying at Berkeley.

While at Berkeley, London continued to study and spend time at Heinold's saloon, where he was introduced to the sailors and adventurers who would influence his writing. In his autobiographical novel, John Barleycorn, London mentioned the pub's likeness seventeen times. Heinold's was the place where London met Alexander McLean, a captain known for his cruelty at sea. London based his protagonist Wolf Larsen, in the novel The Sea-Wolf, on McLean.

Heinold's First and Last Chance Saloon is now unofficially named Jack London's Rendezvous in his honor.

Gold rush and first success

On July 12, 1897, London (age 21) and his sister's husband Captain Shepard sailed to join the Klondike Gold Rush. This was the setting for some of his first successful stories. London's time in the harsh Klondike, however, was detrimental to his health. Like so many other men who were malnourished in the goldfields, London developed scurvy. His gums became swollen, leading to the loss of his four front teeth. A constant gnawing pain affected his hip and leg muscles, and his face was stricken with marks that always reminded him of the struggles he faced in the Klondike. Father William Judge, "The Saint of Dawson", had a facility in Dawson that provided shelter, food and any available medicine to London and others. His struggles there inspired London's short story, "To Build a Fire" (1902, revised in 1908), which many critics assess as his best.

His landlords in Dawson were mining engineers Marshall Latham Bond and Louis Whitford Bond, educated at Yale and Stanford, respectively. The brothers' father, Judge Hiram Bond, was a wealthy mining investor. The Bonds, especially Hiram, were active Republicans. Marshall Bond's diary mentions friendly sparring with London on political issues as a camp pastime.

London left Oakland with a social conscience and socialist leanings; he returned to become an activist for socialism. He concluded that his only hope of escaping the work "trap" was to get an education and "sell his brains". He saw his writing as a business, his ticket out of poverty, and, he hoped, a means of beating the wealthy at their own game. On returning to California in 1898, London began working to get published, a struggle described in his novel, Martin Eden (serialized in 1908, published in 1909). His first published story since high school was "To the Man On Trail", which has frequently been collected in anthologies. When The Overland Monthly offered him only five dollars for it—and was slow paying—London came close to abandoning his writing career. In his words, "literally and literarily I was saved" when The Black Cat accepted his story "A Thousand Deaths", and paid him $40—the "first money I ever received for a story".

London began his writing career just as new printing technologies enabled lower-cost production of magazines. This resulted in a boom in popular magazines aimed at a wide public audience and a strong market for short fiction. In 1900, he made $2,500 in writing, about $75,000 in today's currency. Among the works he sold to magazines was a short story known as either "Diable" (1902) or "Bâtard" (1904), two editions of the same basic story; London received $141.25 for this story on May 27, 1902. In the text, a cruel French Canadian brutalizes his dog, and the dog retaliates and kills the man. London told some of his critics that man's actions are the main cause of the behavior of their animals, and he would show this in another story, The Call of the Wild.

In early 1903, London sold The Call of the Wild to The Saturday Evening Post for $750, and the book rights to Macmillan for $2,000. Macmillan's promotional campaign propelled it to swift success.

While living at his rented villa on Lake Merritt in Oakland, California, London met poet George Sterling; in time they became best friends. In 1902, Sterling helped London find a home closer to his own in nearby Piedmont. In his letters London addressed Sterling as "Greek", owing to Sterling's aquiline nose and classical profile, and he signed them as "Wolf". London was later to depict Sterling as Russ Brissenden in his autobiographical novel Martin Eden (1910) and as Mark Hall in The Valley of the Moon (1913).

In later life London indulged his wide-ranging interests by accumulating a personal library of 15,000 volumes. He referred to his books as "the tools of my trade".

First marriage (1900–04)

London married Elizabeth "Bessie" Maddern on April 7, 1900, the same day The Son of the Wolf was published. Bess had been part of his circle of friends for a number of years. She was related to stage actresses Minnie Maddern Fiske and Emily Stevens. Stasz says, "Both acknowledged publicly that they were not marrying out of love, but from friendship and a belief that they would produce sturdy children." Kingman says, "they were comfortable together... Jack had made it clear to Bessie that he did not love her, but that he liked her enough to make a successful marriage."

London met Bessie through his friend at Oakland High School, Fred Jacobs; she was Fred's fiancee. Bessie, who tutored at Anderson's University Academy in Alameda California, tutored Jack in preparation for his entrance exams for the University of California at Berkeley in 1896. Jacobs was killed aboard the USAT Scandia in 1897, but Jack and Bessie continued their friendship, which included taking photos and developing the film together. This was the beginning of Jack's passion for photography.

During the marriage, London continued his friendship with Anna Strunsky, co-authoring The Kempton-Wace Letters, an epistolary novel contrasting two philosophies of love. Anna, writing "Dane Kempton's" letters, arguing for a romantic view of marriage, while London, writing "Herbert Wace's" letters, argued for a scientific view, based on Darwinism and eugenics. In the novel, his fictional character contrasted two women he had known.

London's pet name for Bess was "Mother-Girl" and Bess's for London was "Daddy-Boy". Their first child, Joan, was born on January 15, 1901, and their second, Bessie (later called Becky), on October 20, 1902. Both children were born in Piedmont, California. Here London wrote one of his most celebrated works, The Call of the Wild.

While London had pride in his children, the marriage was strained. Kingman says that by 1903 the couple were close to separation as they were "extremely incompatible". "Jack was still so kind and gentle with Bessie that when Cloudsley Johns was a house guest in February 1903 he didn't suspect a breakup of their marriage."

London reportedly complained to friends Joseph Noel and George Sterling:

[Bessie] is devoted to purity. When I tell her morality is only evidence of low blood pressure, she hates me. She'd sell me and the children out for her damned purity. It's terrible. Every time I come back after being away from home for a night she won't let me be in the same room with her if she can

198

help it.

Stasz writes that these were "code words for [Bess's] fear that [Jack] was consorting with prostitutes and might bring home venereal disease."

On July 24, 1903, London told Bessie he was leaving and moved out. During 1904, London and Bess negotiated the terms of a divorce, and the decree was granted on November 11, 1904.

War correspondent (1904)

London accepted an assignment of the San Francisco Examiner to cover the Russo-Japanese War in early 1904, arriving in Yokohama on January 25, 1904. He was arrested by Japanese authorities in Shimonoseki, but released through the intervention of American ambassador Lloyd Griscom. After travelling to Korea, he was again arrested by Japanese authorities for straying too close to the border with Manchuria without official permission, and was sent back to Seoul. Released again, London was permitted to travel with the Imperial Japanese Army to the border, and to observe the Battle of the Yalu.

London asked William Randolph Hearst, the owner of the San Francisco Examiner, to be allowed to transfer to the Imperial Russian Army, where he felt that restrictions on his reporting and his movements would be less severe. However, before this could be arranged, he was arrested for a third time in four months, this time for assaulting his Japanese assistants, whom he accused of stealing the fodder for his horse. Released through the personal intervention of President Theodore Roosevelt, London departed the front in June 1904.

Bohemian Club

On August 18, 1904, London went with his close friend, the poet George Sterling, to "Summer High Jinks" at the Bohemian Grove. London was elected to honorary membership in the Bohemian Club and took part in many activities. Other noted members of the Bohemian Club during this time included Ambrose Bierce, Gelett Burgess, Allan Dunn, John Muir, Frank Norris, and Herman George Scheffauer.

Beginning in December 1914, London worked on The Acorn Planter, A California Forest Play, to be performed as one of the annual Grove Plays, but it was never selected. It was described as too difficult to set to music. London published The Acorn Planter in 1916.

Second marriage

After divorcing Maddern, London married Charmian Kittredge in 1905. London was introduced to Kittredge in 1900 by her aunt Netta Eames, who was an editor at Overland Monthly magazine in San Francisco. The two met prior to his first marriage but became lovers years later after Jack and Bessie London visited Wake Robin, Netta Eames' Sonoma County resort, in 1903. London was injured when he fell from a buggy, and Netta arranged for Charmian to care for him. The two developed a friendship, as Charmian, Netta, her husband Roscoe, and London were politically aligned with socialist causes. At some point the relationship became romantic, and Jack divorced his wife to marry Charmian, who was five years his senior.

Biographer Russ Kingman called Charmian "Jack's soul-mate, always at his side, and a perfect match." Their time together included numerous trips, including a 1907 cruise on the yacht Snark to Hawaii and Australia. Many of London's stories are based on his visits to Hawaii, the last one for 10 months beginning in December 1915.

The couple also visited Goldfield, Nevada, in 1907, where they were guests of the Bond brothers, London's Dawson City landlords. The Bond brothers were working in Nevada as mining engineers.

London had contrasted the concepts of the "Mother Girl" and the "Mate Woman" in The Kempton-Wace Letters. His pet name for Bess had been "Mother-Girl;" his pet name for Charmian was "Mate-Woman." Charmian's aunt and foster mother, a disciple of Victoria Woodhull, had raised her without prudishness. Every biographer alludes to Charmian's uninhibited sexuality.

Joseph Noel calls the events from 1903 to 1905 "a domestic drama that would have intrigued the pen of an Ibsen.... London's had comedy relief in it and a sort of easy-going romance." In broad outline, London was restless in his first marriage, sought extramarital sexual affairs, and found, in Charmian Kittredge, not only a sexually active and adventurous partner, but his future life-companion. They attempted to have children; one child died at birth, and another pregnancy ended in a miscarriage.

In 1906, London published in Collier's magazine his eye-witness report of the San Francisco earthquake.

Beauty Ranch (1905–16)

In 1905, London purchased a 1,000 acres (4.0 km2) ranch in Glen Ellen, Sonoma County, California, on the eastern slope of Sonoma Mountain, for $26,450. He wrote: "Next to my wife, the ranch is the dearest thing in the world to me." He desperately wanted the ranch to become a successful business enterprise. Writing, always a commercial enterprise with London, now became even more a means to an end: "I write for no other purpose than to add to the beauty that now belongs to me. I write a book for no other reason than to add three or four hundred acres to my magnificent estate."

Stasz writes that London "had taken fully to heart the vision, expressed in his agrarian fiction, of the land as the closest earthly version of Eden ... he educated himself through the study of agricultural manuals and scientific tomes. He conceived of a system of ranching that today would be praised for its ecological wisdom." He was proud to own the first concrete silo in California, a circular piggery that he designed. He hoped to adapt the wisdom of Asian sustainable agriculture to the United States. He hired both Italian and Chinese stonemasons, whose distinctly different styles are obvious.

The ranch was an economic failure. Sympathetic observers such as Stasz treat his projects as potentially feasible, and ascribe their failure to bad luck or to being ahead of their time. Unsympathetic historians such as Kevin Starr suggest that he was a bad manager, distracted by other concerns and impaired by his alcoholism. Starr notes that London was absent from his ranch about six months a year between 1910 and 1916 and says, "He liked the show of managerial power, but not grinding attention to detail .... London's workers laughed at his efforts to play big-time rancher [and considered] the operation a rich man's hobby."

London spent $80,000 ($2,230,000 in current value) to build a 15,000-square-foot (1,400 m2) stone mansion called Wolf House on the property. Just as the mansion was nearing completion, two weeks before the Londons planned to move in, it was destroyed by fire.

London's last visit to Hawaii, beginning in December 1915, lasted eight months. He met with Duke Kahanamoku, Prince Jonah Kūhiō Kalaniana'ole, Queen Lili'uokalani and many others, before returning to his ranch in July 1916. He was suffering from kidney failure, but he continued to work.

The ranch (abutting stone remnants of Wolf House) is now a National Historic Landmark and is protected in Jack London State Historic Park.

Animal activism

London witnessed animal cruelty in the training of circus animals, and his subsequent novels Jerry of the Islands and Michael, Brother of Jerry included a foreword entreating the public to become more informed about this practice. In 1918, the Massachusetts Society for the Prevention of Cruelty to Animals and the American Humane Education Society teamed up to create the Jack London Club, which sought to inform the public about cruelty to circus animals and encourage them to protest this establishment. Support from Club members led to a temporary cessation of trained animal acts at Ringling-Barnum and Bailey in 1925.

Death

London died November 22, 1916, in a sleeping porch in a cottage on his ranch. London had been a robust man but had suffered several serious illnesses, including scurvy in the Klondike. Additionally, during travels on the Snark, he and Charmian picked up unspecified tropical infections, and diseases, including yaws. At the time of his death, he suffered from dysentery, late-stage alcoholism, and uremia; he was in extreme pain and taking morphine.

202

London's ashes were buried on his property not far from the Wolf House. London's funeral took place on November 26, 1916, attended only by close friends, relatives, and workers of the property. In accordance with his wishes, he was cremated and buried next to some pioneer children, under a rock that belonged to the Wolf House. After Charmian's death in 1955, she was also cremated and then buried with her husband in the same simple spot that her husband chose. The grave is marked by a mossy boulder. The buildings and property were later preserved as Jack London State Historic Park, in Glen Ellen, California.

Suicide debate

Because he was using morphine, many older sources describe London's death as a suicide, and some still do. This conjecture appears to be a rumor, or speculation based on incidents in his fiction writings. His death certificate gives the cause as uremia, following acute renal colic.

The biographer Stasz writes, "Following London's death, for a number of reasons, a biographical myth developed in which he has been portrayed as an alcoholic womanizer who committed suicide. Recent scholarship based upon firsthand documents challenges this caricature." Most biographers, including Russ Kingman, now agree he died of uremia aggravated by an accidental morphine overdose.

London's fiction featured several suicides. In his autobiographical memoir John Barleycorn, he claims, as a youth, to have drunkenly stumbled overboard into the San Francisco Bay, "some maundering fancy of going out with the tide suddenly obsessed me". He said he drifted and nearly succeeded in drowning before sobering up and being rescued by fishermen. In the dénouement of The Little Lady of the Big House, the heroine, confronted by the pain of a mortal gunshot wound, undergoes a physician-assisted suicide by morphine. Also, in Martin Eden, the principal protagonist, who shares certain characteristics with London, drowns himself.

Accusations of plagiarism

London was vulnerable to accusations of plagiarism, both because he was such a conspicuous, prolific, and successful writer and because of his methods of working. He wrote in a letter to Elwyn Hoffman, "expression, you see—with me—is far easier than invention." He purchased plots and novels from the young Sinclair Lewis and used incidents from newspaper clippings as writing material.

In July 1901, two pieces of fiction appeared within the same month: London's "Moon-Face", in the San Francisco Argonaut, and Frank Norris' "The Passing of Cock-eye Blacklock", in Century Magazine. Newspapers showed the similarities between the stories, which London said were "quite different in manner of treatment, [but] patently the same in foundation and motive." London explained both writers based their stories on the same newspaper account. A year later, it was discovered that Charles Forrest McLean had published a fictional story also based on the same incident.

Egerton Ryerson Young claimed The Call of the Wild (1903) was taken from Young's book My Dogs in the Northland (1902). London acknowledged using it as a source and claimed to have written a letter to Young thanking him.

In 1906, the New York World published "deadly parallel" columns showing eighteen passages from London's short story "Love of Life" side by side with similar passages from a nonfiction article by Augustus Biddle and J. K. Macdonald, titled "Lost in the Land of the Midnight Sun". London noted the World did not accuse him of "plagiarism", but only of "identity of time and situation", to which he defiantly "pled guilty".

The most serious charge of plagiarism was based on London's "The Bishop's Vision", Chapter 7 of his novel The Iron Heel (1908). The chapter is nearly identical to an ironic essay that Frank Harris published in 1901, titled "The Bishop of London and Public Morality". Harris was incensed and suggested he should receive 1/60th of the royalties from The Iron Heel, the disputed material constituting about that fraction of the whole novel. London insisted he had clipped a reprint of the article, which had appeared in an American newspaper, and believed it to be a genuine speech delivered by the Bishop of London.

Views

Atheism

London was an atheist. He is quoted as saying, "I believe that when I am dead, I am dead. I believe that with my death I am just as much obliterated as the last mosquito you and I squashed."

Socialism

London wrote from a socialist viewpoint, which is evident in his novel The Iron Heel. Neither a theorist nor an intellectual socialist, London's socialism grew out of his life experience. As London explained in his essay, "How I Became a Socialist", his views were influenced by his experience with people at the bottom of the social pit. His optimism and individualism faded, and he vowed never to do more hard physical work than necessary. He wrote that his individualism was hammered out of him, and he was politically reborn. He often closed his letters "Yours for the Revolution."

London joined the Socialist Labor Party in April 1896. In the same year, the San Francisco Chronicle published a story about the twenty-year-old London's giving nightly speeches in Oakland's City Hall Park, an activity he was arrested for a year later. In 1901, he left the Socialist Labor Party and joined the new Socialist Party of America. He ran unsuccessfully as the high-profile Socialist candidate for mayor of Oakland in 1901 (receiving 245 votes) and 1905 (improving to 981 votes), toured the country lecturing on socialism in 1906, and published two collections of essays about socialism: The War of the Classes (1905) and Revolution, and other Essays (1906).

Stasz notes that "London regarded the Wobblies as a welcome addition to the Socialist cause, although he never joined them in going so far as to recommend sabotage." Stasz mentions a personal meeting between London and Big Bill Haywood in 1912.

In his late (1913) book The Cruise of the Snark, London writes about appeals to him for membership of the Snark's crew from office workers and other "toilers" who longed for escape from the cities, and of being cheated by workmen.

In his Glen Ellen ranch years, London felt some ambivalence toward socialism and complained about the "inefficient Italian labourers" in his employ. In 1916, he resigned from the Glen Ellen chapter of the Socialist Party, but stated emphatically he did so "because of its lack of fire and fight, and its loss of emphasis on the class struggle." In an unflattering portrait of London's ranch days, California cultural historian Kevin Starr refers to this period as "post-socialist" and says "... by 1911 ... London was more bored by the class struggle than he cared to admit."

Racial views

London shared common concerns among European Americans in California about Asian immigration, described as "the yellow peril"; he used the latter term as the title of a 1904 essay. This theme was also the subject of a story he wrote in 1910 called "The Unparalleled Invasion". Presented as an historical essay set in the future, the story narrates events between 1976 and 1987, in which China, with an ever-increasing population, is taking over and colonizing its neighbors with the intention of taking over the entire Earth. The western nations respond with biological warfare and bombard China with dozens of the most infectious diseases. On his fears about China, he admits, "it must be taken into consideration that the above postulate is itself a product of Western race-egotism, urged by our belief in our own righteousness and fostered by a faith in ourselves which may be as erroneous as are most fond race fancies."

By contrast, many of London's short stories are notable for their empathetic portrayal of Mexican ("The Mexican"), Asian ("The Chinago"), and Hawaiian ("Koolau the Leper") characters. London's war correspondence from the Russo-Japanese War, as well as his unfinished novel Cherry, show he admired much about Japanese customs and capabilities. London's writings have been popular among the Japanese, who believe he portrayed them positively.

In "Koolau the Leper", London describes Koolau, who is a Hawaiian leper—and thus a very different sort of "superman" than Martin Eden—and who fights off an entire cavalry troop to elude capture, as "indomitable spiritually—a ... magnificent rebel". This character is based on Hawaiian leper Kaluaikoolau, who in 1893 revolted and resisted capture from forces of the Provisional Government of Hawaii in the Kalalau Valley.

An amateur boxer and avid boxing fan, London reported on the 1910 Johnson–Jeffries fight, in which the black boxer Jack Johnson vanquished Jim Jeffries, known as the "Great White Hope". In 1908, London had reported on an earlier fight of Johnson's, contrasting the black boxer's coolness and intellectual style, with the apelike appearance and fighting style of his Canadian opponent, Tommy Burns,

'what ... [won] on Saturday was bigness, coolness, quickness, cleverness, and vast physical superiority... Because a white man wishes a white man to win, this should not prevent him from giving absolute credit to the best man, even when that best man was black. All hail to Johnson.' London wrote that Johnson was 'superb. He was impregnable . . . as inaccessible as Mont Blanc.'

Those who defend London against charges of racism cite the letter he wrote to the Japanese-American Commercial Weekly in 1913:

In reply to yours of August 16, 1913. First of all, I should say by stopping the stupid newspaper from always fomenting race prejudice. This of course, being impossible, I would say, next, by educating the people of Japan so that they will be too intelligently tolerant to respond to any call to race prejudice. And, finally, by realizing, in industry and government, of socialism—which last word is merely a word that stands for the actual application of in the affairs of men of the theory of the Brotherhood of Man.

In the meantime the nations and races are only unruly boys who have not yet grown to the stature of men. So we must expect them to do unruly and boisterous things at times. And, just as boys grow up, so the races of mankind will grow up and laugh when they look back upon their childish quarrels.

In 1996, after the City of Whitehorse, Yukon, renamed a street in honor

207

of London, protests over London's alleged racism forced the city to change the name of "Jack London Boulevard" back to "Two-mile Hill".

Works

Short stories

Western writer and historian Dale L. Walker writes:

London's true métier was the short story ... London's true genius lay in the short form, 7,500 words and under, where the flood of images in his teeming brain and the innate power of his narrative gift were at once constrained and freed. His stories that run longer than the magic 7,500 generally—but certainly not always—could have benefited from self-editing.

London's "strength of utterance" is at its height in his stories, and they are painstakingly well-constructed. "To Build a Fire" is the best known of all his stories. Set in the harsh Klondike, it recounts the haphazard trek of a new arrival who has ignored an old-timer's warning about the risks of traveling alone. Falling through the ice into a creek in seventy-five-below weather, the unnamed man is keenly aware that survival depends on his untested skills at quickly building a fire to dry his clothes and warm his extremities. After publishing a tame version of this story—with a sunny outcome—in The Youth's Companion in 1902, London offered a second, more severe take on the man's predicament in The Century Magazine in 1908. Reading both provides an illustration of London's growth and maturation as a writer. As Labor (1994) observes: "To compare the two versions is itself an instructive lesson in what distinguished a great work of literary art from a good children's story."

Other stories from the Klondike period include: "All Gold Canyon", about a battle between a gold prospector and a claim jumper; "The Law of Life", about an aging American Indian man abandoned by his tribe and left to die; "Love of Life", about a trek by a prospector across the Canadian tundra; "To the Man on Trail," which tells the story of a prospector fleeing the Mounted Police in a sled race, and raises the question of the contrast between written law and morality; and "An Odyssey of the North," which raises questions of conditional morality, and paints a sympathetic portrait of a man of mixed White and Aleut ancestry.

London was a boxing fan and an avid amateur boxer. "A Piece of Steak" is a tale about a match between older and younger boxers. It contrasts the differing experiences of youth and age but also raises the social question of the treatment of aging workers. "The Mexican" combines boxing with a social theme, as a young Mexican endures an unfair fight and ethnic prejudice in order to earn money with which to aid the revolution.

Several of London's stories would today be classified as science fiction. "The Unparalleled Invasion" describes germ warfare against China; "Goliath" is about an irresistible energy weapon; "The Shadow and the Flash" is a tale about two brothers who take different routes to achieving invisibility; "A Relic of the Pliocene" is a tall tale about an encounter of a modern-day man with a mammoth. "The Red One" is a late story from a period when London was intrigued by the theories of the psychiatrist and writer Jung. It tells of an island tribe held in thrall by an extraterrestrial object.

Some nineteen original collections of short stories were published during London's brief life or shortly after his death. There have been several posthumous anthologies drawn from this pool of stories. Many of these stories were located in the Klondike and the Pacific. A collection of Jack London's San Francisco Stories was published in October 2010 by Sydney Samizdat Press.

Novels

London's most famous novels are The Call of the Wild, White Fang, The Sea-Wolf, The Iron Heel, and Martin Eden.

In a letter dated Dec 27, 1901, London's Macmillan publisher George Platt Brett, Sr., said "he believed Jack's fiction represented 'the very best kind of work' done in America."

Critic Maxwell Geismar called The Call of the Wild "a beautiful prose poem"; editor Franklin Walker said that it "belongs on a shelf with Walden and Huckleberry Finn"; and novelist E.L. Doctorow called it "a mordant parable ... his masterpiece."

The historian Dale L. Walker commented:

Jack London was an uncomfortable novelist, that form too long for his natural impatience and the quickness of his mind. His novels, even the best of them, are hugely flawed.

Some critics have said that his novels are episodic and resemble linked short stories. Dale L. Walker writes:

The Star Rover, that magnificent experiment, is actually a series of short stories connected by a unifying device ... Smoke Bellew is a series of stories bound together in a novel-like form by their reappearing protagonist, Kit Bellew; and John Barleycorn ... is a synoptic series of short episodes.

Ambrose Bierce said of The Sea-Wolf that "the great thing—and it is among the greatest of things—is that tremendous creation, Wolf Larsen ... the hewing out and setting up of such a figure is enough for a man to do in one lifetime." However, he noted, "The love element, with its absurd suppressions, and impossible proprieties, is awful."

The Iron Heel is interesting as an example of a dystopian novel that anticipates and influenced George Orwell's Nineteen Eighty-Four. London's socialist politics are explicitly on display here. The Iron Heel meets the contemporary definition of soft science fiction. The Star Rover (1915) is also science fiction.

Apocrypha

Jack London Credo

London's literary executor, Irving Shepard, quoted a Jack London Credo in an introduction to a 1956 collection of London stories:

I would rather be ashes than dust!

I would rather that my spark should burn out in a brilliant blaze than it should be stifled by dry-rot.

I would rather be a superb meteor, every atom of me in magnificent glow, than a sleepy and permanent planet.

The function of man is to live, not to exist.

I shall not waste my days in trying to prolong them.

I shall use my time.

The biographer Stasz notes that the passage "has many marks of London's style" but the only line that could be safely attributed to London was the first. The words Shepard quoted were from a story in the San Francisco Bulletin, December 2, 1916, by journalist Ernest J. Hopkins, who visited the ranch just weeks before London's death. Stasz notes, "Even more so than today journalists' quotes were unreliable or even sheer inventions," and says no direct source in London's writings has been found. However, at least one line, according to Stasz, is authentic, being referenced by London and written in his own hand in the autograph book of Australian suffragette Vida Goldstein:

Dear Miss Goldstein:–

Seven years ago I wrote you that I'd rather be ashes than dust. I still subscribe to that sentiment.

Sincerely yours,

Jack London

Jan. 13, 1909

Furthermore, in his short story "By The Turtles of Tasman", a character, defending her ne'er-do-well grasshopperish father to her antlike uncle, says: "... my father has been a king. He has lived .... Have you lived merely to live? Are you afraid to die? I'd rather sing one wild song and burst my heart with it, than live a thousand years watching my digestion and being afraid of the wet. When you are dust, my father will be ashes."

"The Scab"

A short diatribe on "The Scab" is often quoted within the U.S. labor movement and frequently attributed to London. It opens:

After God had finished the rattlesnake, the toad, and the vampire, he had some awful substance left with which he made a scab. A scab is a two-legged animal with a corkscrew soul, a water brain, a combination backbone of jelly and glue. Where others have hearts, he carries a tumor of rotten principles. When a scab comes down the street, men turn their backs and Angels weep in Heaven, and the Devil shuts the gates of hell to keep him out....

In 1913 and 1914, a number of newspapers printed the first three sentences with varying terms used instead of "scab", such as "knocker", "stool pigeon" or "scandal monger".

This passage as given above was the subject of a 1974 Supreme Court case, Letter Carriers v. Austin, in which Justice Thurgood Marshall referred to it as "a well-known piece of trade union literature, generally attributed to author Jack London". A union newsletter had published a "list of scabs," which was granted to be factual and therefore not libelous, but then went on to quote the passage as the "definition of a scab". The case turned on the question of whether the "definition" was defamatory. The court ruled that "Jack London's... 'definition of a scab' is merely rhetorical hyperbole, a lusty and imaginative expression of the contempt felt by union members towards those who refuse to join", and as such was not libelous and was protected under the First Amendment.

Despite being frequently attributed to London, the passage does not appear at all in the extensive collection of his writings at Sonoma State University's website. However, in his book The War of the Classes he published a 1903 speech entitled "The Scab", which gave a much more balanced view of the topic:

The laborer who gives more time or strength or skill for the same wage than another, or equal time or strength or skill for a less wage, is a scab. The generousness on his part is hurtful to his fellow-laborers, for it compels them to an equal generousness which is not to their liking, and which gives them less of food and shelter. But a word may be said for the scab. Just as his act makes his rivals compulsorily generous, so do they, by fortune of birth and training, make compulsory his act of generousness.

[...]

Nobody desires to scab, to give most for least. The ambition of every individual is quite the opposite, to give least for most; and, as a result, living in a tooth-and-nail society, battle royal is waged by the ambitious individuals. But in its most salient aspect, that of the struggle over the division of the joint product, it is no longer a battle between individuals, but between groups of individuals. Capital and labor apply themselves to raw material, make something useful out of it, add to its value, and then proceed to quarrel over the division of the added value. Neither cares to give most for least. Each is intent on giving less than the other and on receiving more. (Source: Wikipedia)